Successful Day Nursery Management

Geraldine Jennings

Attic Press
Dublin

© Jennings, Geraldine 1990

First Published in 1990 by
Attic Press
44 East Essex Street
Dublin 2

British Library Cataloguing in Publication Data
Jennings, Geraldine
    Successful day nursery management.
    1. Creches. Organization
    I. Title
    362.712

    ISBN 1-85594-006-X

Cover Design: Concept: Brenda McArdle
Origination: Attic Press
Printing: The Guernsey Press Co Ltd

Acknowledgement

I would like to thank Denise Doyle, Irene Milner and especially my sister Paula Jennings for all their help.

Dedication

To Tamara and David who helped me with my 'puter'.

About the Author

Geraldine Jennings is a highly experienced nursery manager. She worked for several years with children in the USA and in Belgium and on her return to Ireland in 1978 opened *Kinderkare Day Nursery* in Dublin which she ran for nine years. She lives in Dublin and has two children.

Table of Contents

List of Figures

Introduction

Day Nursery Management covers topics as diverse as children's psychological and physical needs, financial planning, marketing and many more. As a day nursery manager, you must try to keep yourself up-to-date on a wide range of topics, from new games for children to the results of the latest studies in quality child care, from personnel relations to developments in tax law.

Wherever a day nursery can be set up, it will almost certainly answer a need. You need not necessarily fear being too near another established nursery because no two nurseries are the same. They each have different staff and a different ethos. Parents also have different expectations of nurseries, so although a number of nurseries may be excellent, different parents will prefer one over another. Choosing a nursery is very personal so although you may not appeal to all of the people all of the time, you should appeal to some of the people some of the time!

It is a big step to open your own nursery and when you do, you may find it difficult to discontinue the business. You will be investing a lot of your time and money, especially in the first few years. Staff and parents will be relying on you: a mother's employment may be dependent on her having arranged reliable child care. A child can become confused if forced, due to closure, to leave a nursery in which s/he is settled and happy. The child may believe that s/he is somehow to blame for the upset caused in the family, especially if the nursery closes at short notice. Your staff may have taken on commitments based on their salary, and so on.

As in any business, most of the day-to-day management and decisions will be yours initially, and only later will you be in a position to delegate some responsibility. It may be a long time before you have enough confidence in your staff to take time off for a holiday. When you do finally arrange a well earned holiday there is always the risk of having to cancel bookings due to unforeseen problems!

In the beginning you will have to put in long hours... You may have children until six o'clock in the evening and when they are gone you may have to attend to the books. All the responsibility is yours and yours alone. You must be as sure as you can be that you have reached the maturity and position in your life that you feel ready to take on the challenge of running a business.

Even if you feel you might prefer to postpone opening the nursery for a few years, any child care courses and the reading you may have done will stand to you now and in the future. You may like to extend your child care experience by further training courses or to gain more experience by working in a nursery. You may feel that, while your child care qualifications are excellent you will benefit from further business studies.

When you are ready to go ahead with your plans to open a day nursery, it will be well worth it. To run any business is challenging and rewarding but this is especially true of running a day nursery because of the immense satisfaction that working with children brings. It contains many diverse aspects of human relationships, both business and personal, and makes for a most fulfilling career.

This book can only be a guide. It is you, your personality and temperament, which will make your nursery unique. Avoid comparing it to other nurseries. Make it the very best you can, a place where you will be proud to welcome children parents and employees.

Before I set up *Kinderkare Day Nursery*, I was not fully convinced that it was in the best interest of a child to spend a portion of the day away from her/his mother but now I feel that a child can benefit enormously from being in *high quality day care*. A day nursery must strive to serve the children in its care first and then to be economically viable without compromising the welfare of the children. It is nothing short of criminal to run a day nursery with the sole motivation of making money at the expense of the children.

Chapter One
The Demand for Child Care

There is a growing demand for a variety of child care facilities. More than ever, working parents are looking for reliable, formal child-minding arrangements. They are no longer content to have an ad hoc arrangement with a neighbour or relation such as the child's grandmother, and frequently grandmothers are less inclined to want to take upon themselves the daily care of another generation of children. Grandparents have a longer life expectancy and have higher expectations for their retiring years. They themselves may well want to become involved in activities outside the home.

Mothers are becoming better informed and are more demanding of what they want from their child care. It is no longer acceptable for someone to receive five or six children into her living room or converted garage and assume the title 'day nursery'. A mother who sends her child to a day nursery will expect the highest standard of care and facilities and she will require that the time her child spends in the nursery environment is positively beneficial and complements the care the child receives at home.

The environment is acknowledged as an important influence on human development. The question of whether environment or heredity is the chief influence is debatable... It is the question of Nurture versus Nature. Environmentalists believe that a child is born as a 'blank computer disc' ready to receive, from the environment, most of the information which will eventually determine her character, for good or for ill.

The environment can be understood as everything and everybody with which the child has contact. Obviously, every child is brought up in some type of environment but it is the richness of the environment, in more than economic terms, which determines its effects. A child may be born into a family which lacks for nothing materially but may be attending a nursery which provides little stimulation. Because the child may spend up to half of her/his young life in the nursery, the nursery will play a key role in the child's life and the quality of the nursery environment is of paramount importance. The nursery has a responsibility to both the physical and the psychological needs of the child. It must strive to do more than simply keep the child safe, clean, dry, warm and fed - quality child care goes very much further than this.

The child's psychological needs are every bit as important as her/his physical needs, although more difficult to identify. Questions will certainly be asked if a child is cold, hungry or dirty when collected by her/his parents. If, on the other hand, a child's basic psychological needs are not met, the deficiencies may not become apparent until the child enters young adulthood. Then the parents may become aware of problems and begin to wonder 'Where did we go wrong?'

For a nursery to respond to the parents and children effectively, the manager must try to understand the needs of her clients and the problems facing working mothers especially.

Child Care and the Family

Once a mother has made the decision to return to paid employment she must then decide how soon after the baby's birth this will be. An increasing number of women are returning to work outside the home shortly after the birth of their child. Maternity leave entitles a mother to up to ten weeks paid leave; four to six weeks before (or after) the birth and four weeks after, plus four weeks unpaid leave.

Women should be realistic about the length of time they need to recover physically after childbirth. It is by no means unusual to feel below par for much longer than six weeks. The stress of childbirth coupled with the demands of the new baby will be exacerbated by the demands of returning to work, and the nursery manager should be sympathetic and as helpful as possible.

Many of us know very well how exhausting a day's work can be without the added demands of a young child. The first thing that has to be done after a day's work is to collect the child, perhaps battling through the rush hour traffic to do so. Once home you can't relax for an hour. You will very likely have to make the evening meal and do other household tasks and still find time to spend with your child before bedtime. Some parents put their babies to bed late so that they can spend more time with them. Tiredness is the most common complaint among the parents of young children - working parents have an even greater cause for complaint.

The nursery staff should encourage parents to discuss any aspect of their child's care, including such issues as feeding or sleeping problems.

Attitudes to Child Care

Some people are quite negative about day care, possibly as a result of assertions made by researchers like John Bowlby, whose study of children deprived of their mothers and raised in an institution led him to state:

> What is believed to be essential to the mental health is that the infant and young child should experience a warm, intimate and continuous relationship with its mother (or permanent mother substitute) in which both find satisfaction and enjoyment.
> *Child Care and the Growth of Love*, 1953

There is a great difference between being deprived of a family - father, mother, siblings - for long periods, as can happen in an institution, and being separated from them for a part of each day. To compare day care with institutional care is not comparing like with like.

Findings indicate unequivocally that children in day care are securely attached to their mothers and this feeling is not replaced by their relationship with a substitute carer. The child can form a relationship with the care giver, preferring her to a stranger, but day care children rarely prefer the carer to their mother. The available data indicate that high quality non-maternal care does not appear to have adverse effects on the child's maternal attachment, intellectual development or social/emotional behaviour (*American Psychologist* April 1980).

It has been a popular misconception that the young child has nothing to gain from experiences other than those stemming directly from the mother. In *Child Care and the Growth of Love* John Bowlby reinforces this erroneous idea when he writes:

> It is against this background that the reason why young children thrive better in bad homes than in good institutions, and why children with bad parents are, apparently unreasonably, so attached to them, can be understood. Those responsible for institutions have sometimes been unwilling to acknowledge that children are often better off in quite bad homes, which is the conclusion of most experienced social workers with mental health training and is borne out by evidence already quoted.

This notion was encouraged by those in authority, as it seemed to imply that a child would be better off at home at all costs. In this way, responsibility for the child's experiences was laid totally at the feet of the parents, especially the mother, conveniently absolving the authorities from any responsibility in assisting in the provision of day care facilities.

When the need for the provision of child care facilities in order to facilitate working mothers is argued, certain groups protest about the lack of job opportunities for men; as if the way to tackle an unemployment problem is to preclude a section of the population, ie women, from the work place. This attitude is quickly reversed when there is a critical shortage of men in the labour force, a fact that was dramatically illustrated during World War 2.

Parents have been encouraged to regard day nurseries as institutions and thus as positively harmful. The results of the early studies of pre-schooling were disappointing. Investigations had shown that the substantial IQ gains associated with good pre-school compensatory education programmes diminish and then disappear within four or five years! The children who had been to pre-school had been initially shown to have benefited intellectually, but within a few years follow-up studies found that there were no substantial differences between recipients and non-recipients of pre-schooling. These results seemed to support John Bowlby's beliefs.

Fortunately later follow-up research has been very much more encouraging. The IQ gains associated with pre-school education which had initially disappeared were found to have been replaced by other socially advantageous characteristics. The findings of one study (*Effects of the Perry Pre-school Program on Youth through age 15*) show that children who attended pre-school have:

* A stronger commitment to schooling and doing well in school than children who did not attend pre-school.
* Higher scores on reading, arithmetic and language achievement tests at all grade levels.
* Stronger commitment to work.

While there is now some evidence to show that children who have had the benefit of good quality pre-school nursery care may gain intellectually and socially, there is no evidence to show that quality day care has any adverse effects on the children or their relationship with their parents. Unfortunately old attitudes die hard and the negative attitudes are still widely held despite recent evidence to the contrary.

The Choice of Child Care

There are two main categories of child care:

Home care
(1)   In child's home:
        By a live-in or daily 'nanny'
(2)   In another person's home

Day Nursery
(1)   Full day care
(2)   Sessional care

No single child-minding arrangement is intrinsically better than another. The family circumstances, likes and dislikes must influence the parents' choice. The age of the child should also be taken into consideration. For a baby under 18 months, a one-to-one arrangement is recommended. A very young baby requires a lot of time and attention and has nothing to gain from being in a large group of babies. If the baby is not a first child it is probably better for all the children in the family to attend the same day care centre - this ensures that the attachment of older and younger brothers and sisters is not harmed. Nurseries must therefore cater for a limited number of infants but with strict limitations on the number of infants attending the day nursery. Many Local Authorities have their own guidelines as to the child/staff ratio for the different types of child care based on the number and ages of the children to be minded.

There is the risk of insufficient supervision and support in the case of a sole child-minder with a number of children. If parents opt for a sole child-minder arrangement, they should confirm that the child-minder is registered with the Local Authority, or, if no such registration system exists, that the child-minder is not taking on too many children. Parents should remember that caring for one infant is difficult, caring for twins can be exasperating but caring for more than two children is difficult enough to warrant help and support. As with day nurseries, child-minders must allow parents unlimited access to their children.

Different parents will have different expectations of nursery care. Some may consider hygiene or nourishment to be of primary importance, while others may stress the importance of the equipment and toys, stability and routines, a warm friendly atmosphere, the child/staff ratio and so on. The children who attend a nursery will spend most of their day in that environment, and the day nursery manager is the adult who will become responsible for the children's welfare. It is parents' duty and right to know as much as possible about the nursery, its staff, and how and with whom the children will spend most of their day.

If parents are shy about asking questions the day nursery manager must be confident about volunteering information. The more the parents know about the nursery the more confident they will be and their increased confidence will influence the child's ability to settle in. Parents don't want to give the impression of lacking confidence in the nursery manager's abilities, nor do they want to seem too fussy so it is often up to the nursery managers to tell them about policy and the daily routing (*See Chapter Thirteen*).

Chapter Two
The Premises

Some Local Authorities have requirements for day nurseries in their area. It is suggested that these regulations be examined in conjunction with the following recommendations.

Each nursery is different partly due to the individual constraints of the building. The size, shape, number of floors and the number of rooms will determine the age of the children to be catered for, the range of ages and ultimately the number and qualifications of staff required. It is impossible to suggest the blueprint for the typical day nursery but here we examine the main features of an ideal day nursery premises.

There are two main types of day nursery premises: **purpose built** and **converted** premises. Because the demand for nurseries tends to be in built-up areas, purpose built day nurseries are the exception rather than the rule. Purpose built premises can be prohibitively expensive for the individual private day nursery owner. The funds available for structural changes when converting premises may be limited so the premises must be basically suitable for conversion for day nursery use. If premises are unsuitable, they can be very difficult to manage and supervise. In the long run if you compromise on the premises, it will make life strained for you, your staff and children. For example, the children may be confined to small rooms, or the rooms might be so large that noise is a problem. There may be too many rooms or stairs for staff to comfortably supervise.

When evaluating premises for use as a day nursery remember that some features are crucial, others are desirable. For example, it is *essential* that the building has adequate accessible exits (in case of an emergency), while it is *desirable* that there be child-sized toilets.

General Requirements

* *Direct Access* from the street to the premises should be avoided if clients are likely to be arriving with their children in cars. There should be some off-street parking to avoid disrupting traffic and endangering the children. If cars have to stop on the side of a busy road they run some risk of causing an accident either to themselves or others. There should be a guarded

crossing if parents and children have to cross a busy street to enter the premises. Ramps are recommended to facilitate prams or wheelchairs.

* The day nursery should ideally be on the *ground level* with no steps or stairs. Accidents on stairs can happen either to toddlers or staff carrying children up or down. If, for example, the toilet is on another floor this can result in at least one member of staff spending the day guiding children to and from the toilet. This does not lead to a high level of job satisfaction for the staff, nor does it foster independence in the children. While some children might feel capable of tackling the stairs, the more frequently they are used the higher the risk of accident. Alternatively, if the day nursery must be on an upper floor, it should be confined to one floor level with access to the garden and fire exits. Depending on the size of the nursery, at least one full accessible fire exit will be necessary.

* It is vital that the day nursery is *adequate in size* to accommodate a range of activities for the children and also has space for necessary equipment storage. It should not, however, be so large that the nursery becomes too institutional. Large buildings tend to be difficult and expensive to heat and can be quite noisy. Children have a passion for running in large spaces, stamping their feet and shouting exuberantly. And why not? But it can lead to accidents, headaches and frayed nerves. (See *Play Area*.)

* The outer entrance will require a soft sprung slow action *self-closing device*. This helps to reduce the likelihood of the cry "Who forgot to close the door? Kate is gone!" An intercom with a door release is highly desirable. It may be preferable that the caller can be seen before being admitted, as it is not always possible to identify a person's voice over an intercom. A second door, half door or gate should also be fitted inside the main door. This reduces the risk of a child leaving while others are arriving. This door must be fitted with a child-proof lock which can still be easily opened by adults in case of emergency. A latch positioned high on the door can be a good solution.

* *Half-doors* may be suitable in many parts of the premises, though the fire officer will not accept them in areas such as the kitchen. Half-doors have the advantage of permitting staff to supervise children who, for example, have to leave the play area to go to the toilet. In case of emergency, one member of staff can supervise two play areas. As children will be in and out

constantly in good weather, inset coir mats are a good idea at all entrances. Alternatively, non-slip dust mats may be suitable and these are available from and serviced by laundry contractors.

* *Storage space* in the nursery for coats, bags, toys and prams is indispensable. If you do not allow for storage you will soon find your office becoming cluttered with everything from bulk purchases to dismantled climbing frames and equipment in need of a nut and bolt. When considering storage space, a good rule-of-thumb is to think of a generous amount and then double it - you still might not have enough space for all the provisions and toys out of circulation!

* *Individual coat hooks* must be fitted and should be of such a design and height that children will not be injured by them. Children will require individual lockers or pigeon-holes for personal items such as a change of clothes for use in the event of an accident. A pram area may be needed for the use of parents who walk to the centre with their child. This storage should be near the door to prevent children playing with prams or doing possible damage to interior walls.

* It is essential that the *play area* be separate, spacious and colourful. A minimum of 2.5 square metres (approx 25 square feet) of play space per child is recommended. Circulation areas such as hallways and corridors should not be included in calculating play space. It is desirable that at least two separate play areas be provided so that active play will not encroach on quiet activities. All play areas must have good natural light with adequate artificial back-up. The ambient temperature of the room may need to be higher than normal household temperatures.

* An open plan arrangement is not really suitable for a day nursery as each child will need a *home base* where s/he can feel secure, can identify with the staff located there and where s/he will not be surrounded by too many children. The play areas should be conducive to both floor play and 'messy' play (i.e. art, water and sand play). In a situation where the play room is very large, it should be divided into distinct *Work Areas*, with each activity having its own territory. For example, there may be a Block and Construction area, a Home area, an Art and Messy area, a Quiet and Reading area, a Nature area, a Music and Movement area. Areas can be defined by suitable furniture, movable screens, sound-absorbing partitions or changes in floor and/or wall finishes. Deep toy storage units which are not easily

overturned can also be used to demarcate areas. The toys required for the particular area can be stored on these shelves. Movable screens should be on a broad base and should be low enough to enable staff to see over them, while giving the children an illusion of privacy. Varied floor surfaces are quite effective, for example using carpet in the reading area, a washable floor covering in the Messy area, and a combination of carpet and hard surface in the Block and Construction area.

* It is desirable that the play room leads directly on to an *external paved surface*. The threshold should be ramped rather than have steps so that the younger children can move freely outdoors and indoors. If part of this outside space can be sheltered children can play outside even in winter.

* *A garden* area is a prerequisite. It should be spacious with plenty of light and little vegetation which could scratch or poke a child's eyes. An area of the garden should be reserved for children to grow flowers and vegetables in slightly raised or cordoned off beds. A messy area for sand or water play is necessary and should be positioned where it will not interrupt the circulation of children. The sand pit must be covered so that it is not soiled by cats straying into the garden. A mix of grass and paving or paths on which the children can ride tricycles is very important. The garden walls must not be climbable and any steep falls and exits should be cordoned off. Swings are quite dangerous and should be partitioned off from other areas and constantly supervised when in use. Climbing apparatus, swings and slides should be fixed on an area of grass. There should be outside storage for equipment. The storage area can have perspex windows, a half door, and other safety features so that the children can use it as a 'Shop' or house while the toys are in use in the garden!

* *Outdoor equipment* can be prohibitively expensive while a little imagination in the planning of the garden can save a lot of money and be more interesting than any one piece of equipment. For example, a large plank or pole on the ground can become a bus, train or walking beam. A bike path which meanders around the garden is much more interesting for the children than going round in circles in a yard. An area which is sunny can be useful for babies and toddlers but it must be possible to screen the babies from strong sunshine. As this is not a frequent problem, a blanket hung from a simple clothes-line at a suitable height can be used as a screen.

* It is not advisable to have the garden accessible to the public area, as gates can be left open by callers. If the garden is not large then a fire-exit may be required and this gate should be opened only in emergencies.

* There should be a *separate sleeping room* for the smaller children and ideally this should be in a quieter part of the building. The room must be adequately ventilated, spacious and cheerful. Even though the children will be asleep most of the time they are there, it is not necessary to darken the room and paint it like the proverbial 'Black Hole of Calcutta'. It can be cheerful without being gaudy. There may be a blind or curtain on the window but it should allow enough light into the room to allow the children to see the mobiles and pictures. It is vital that there is good spacing between cots so as to avoid children disturbing one another by pulling blankets.

* It is a good idea that very young babies use their own *carry-cot*. The familiar home smells on the blankets can make the baby feel secure and this also helps the parents to retain responsibility and confidence in the child's hygienic sleeping conditions. Each baby should have a cot and bed linen for her/his exclusive use to prevent cross-infection.

* The sleeping room must be linked to all parts of the building by a baby alarm. The baby alarm is not intended to replace regular checking of the children. Babies who wake up should not be left in the sleeping room. The babies' sleeping room should be just that: a sleeping room. Unless babies are taken up as soon as they wake they will become conditioned to cry out to be taken up. Children who are not confident that they will be lifted quickly will panic when they awake and will cry immediately. On the other hand children who are relaxed will not be inclined to panic even if they hear you quietly moving about the room. They can be confident that their turn will come and so they may doze off again.

* Within the daily time-table, some *rest time* must be allocated to meet the needs of each child. Some children will require a rest in the afternoon but are too old to sleep in cots. It is unsafe to leave children with babies and so they cannot be let nap in the room with the cots. For these older children, small foam rest mattresses can be used. The mattresses can be piled up to form a divan/sofa with cushions in the quiet area. This solves the storage problem and provides useful extra play material. These mattresses should be of fire resistant foam, with waterproof

fixed cover and detachable washable covers.

* The *cooking area* must be inaccessible to the children. It should lead directly into the dining area and the food can then be served through a serving hatch. This means that children cannot collide with someone bringing hot food from the kitchen to the dining room. In an open plan arrangement, such as a combined kitchen and dining room, the cooking area must be divided off from the dining area to prevent a child coming into contact with the cooker or person preparing hot food.

* It is very difficult to prepare a full dinner for the children and staff on one cooker ring! While you will not require an industrial-sized cooker, you will certainly need an oven.

* Though children must not have access to the *food preparation area*, it should nonetheless be as safe as possible in case a child does stray in. Storage areas and cupboards must be out of the reach of the children. Fridges and cupboards can be fitted with child-proof locks which are available specifically for this purpose. There should be no trailing flexes, curled flexes should be fitted to all electrical items in all parts of the building. Cooker guards should be fitted and precautions be taken that saucepan handles are not left protruding over the edge.

* The *Dining area* should be bright and cheerful. Bright colours such as red and orange are used in restaurants as they have a psychologically stimulating effect. All the dining room furniture should be child-sized. High chairs are not recommended as it is better that younger children sit at the table with the other children on low chairs designed for the purpose. Table tops and work surfaces must be easily cleaned. Formica may not be as pretty as a real oak table but it is easier to keep clean and sterile. It is not advisable to use table cloths as they can be too easily pulled, which can result in a child being injured or scalded by a falling item or slipping on a wet floor.

* Full-time children should be provided with a main meal and morning and afternoon snacks. The nutritional needs of the child should be the primary consideration when planning the menu. The diet should be balanced with a variety of meat, vegetables, eggs, fish, fruit and dairy produce (See chapter on *Food*).

* *Toilets and wash-hand basins* must be suitable or made suitable for the under five year-olds. Step-ups will be required if low bowls are not practicable. Adequate washing facilities are essential with hot water which is thermostatically controlled and not too hot. Potties and trainer seats will be needed for the

younger children. Each training child should have her/his own. Individual or disposable hand-drying towels should be supplied.

* *The toilet and changing area* is required by planning regulations to open off a corridor so that there is a 'ventilation lobby' between group areas and toilet area. There must also be good external ventilation. The toilet should be easily supervised and half-doors are ideal. If possible, WC cubicles should have gravity action saloon doors without a locking device.

* *The changing area* must be separate from all other rooms but may be adjoining or within the toilet area. The changing table should be enclosed on at least two sides, possibly positioned against a wall. While this will reduce the risk of the child falling off the changing table s/he must never be left unattended. The surface must be easily cleaned or ideally covered with a disposable cover.

* Cloth nappies are not practical in a day nursery, but if they are used a separate sluice room will be required. Children must not have access to the sluice room. Lined nappy bins must be provided for disposable nappies. The sealed bag of nappies must be deposited in a bin outside the building after every three or four changes. A bag of soiled nappies must not be left in the building for long periods. There must be a wash hand basin within reach of the changing table. A small bath with a shower attachment may be provided for emergency clean-ups. Many children resist being bathed or showered so if they needs a wash they should not be required to undress completely and should be involved as much as possible in the process to avoid embarrassing them. For example, they may be encouraged to hold the shower, and to soap themselves.

* *Heat and Light*: The centre should be well heated, preferably by water filled radiators, electric storage heaters, or otherwise by oil filled heaters, electrically heated. Convector and fan heaters are less acceptable as they cause dryness in the air. Radiant electric heaters, gas or oil burning heaters are dangerous for the children and must not be used. All heating units have the disadvantage that they are usually indented and have corners which could cause injury to children if they were to fall against them. Modern radiators are less dangerous but where necessary they can be enclosed in a vented casing. All heaters should have guards which are designed so that nothing can be left on top of them. When buying a heater always take expert advice from the selling agent. Generally, open fires should not be used, but if

they are, they must have a spark guard and a fire guard and be under constant supervision. The nursery should have sufficient natural light with adequate artificial lighting when required.

* *Electric sockets* must not be left exposed. Socket covers are available from many department stores.
* Children must not have access to any *windows* which are open or capable of being opened. Windows which will be required to be open for ventilation should be above child level. Low windows must be covered with protective grills. To avoid making the room look like a prison, the protective grills should be decorative, but designed so that children cannot climb up them. Glass doors are not desirable in a day nursery but if there are patio doors at child level these should be made of toughened glass and covered with special protective film.
* *Fire extinguishers* and a fire blanket must be provided.
* *Walls and Floors* Whatever the colour scheme of your nursery, the wall colour will often be obliterated by posters and children's paintings. The lower section of the walls may be lined with fire-resistant cladding which will be immune to damage by toys. This cladding can be continued to dado height (ie to about waist level) with artwork limited to the area above. The artwork zone will require frequent redecorating and though Blu-tack can limit the damage done by frequent moving and removing of paintings, ensure that young children do not put it in their mouths.
* The *floor covering* is the principal element in any interior scheme. The finish is critical from the point of view of safety, serviceability and durability. It can be heavy duty carpeting in areas where children might be playing on the floor, and slip-resistant, washable in other areas.
* All *furniture* must be approved under the latest fire regulations for flammable materials. Furniture must be child-sized and of solid construction, it must not be easily turned over and rounded corners are essential. In the short-term, adult-sized furniture can be modified to suit the children's requirements. It is not advisable that furniture be painted as paintwork gets scratched and requires a large amount of upkeep, but if it is, then non-toxic paint must be used. Natural materials are more appealing.
* Staff should be aware of general and personal *hygiene*. The nursery equipment, fittings and toys should be thoroughly disinfected regularly. Smoking must not be allowed on the premises except at break times in the staff room or out of doors.

* There must be *laundry facilities* for washing and drying bed clothes, children's clothes and so on. The parents should be advised to mark their children's clothes and should not allow them to wear long ribbons and hair clips if they are to be in the company of younger children who are prone to swallow small items.

Planning Permission

Planning Permission is legally required for any development or extension to a building, or for a change in use of a building. It is strongly recommended that any proposed day nursery development have planning permission. It would be very unwise to undertake all the expense of setting up a day nursery only to fall foul of planning laws.

When contemplating opening a nursery, the first thing you should do is contact your local planning officer, who will be able to give you some general advice and guidelines as to the type, location and size of building most likely to comply with the planning regulations in your area. S/he will also advise you on how to make a clear, unambiguous planning application.

While each application is considered on its own merits, some planning authorities and town planners may have preferences for nurseries in one location rather than another. For example permission may be difficult to obtain in an area which is felt to be well serviced by child care facilities. Planning Permission is unlikely to be granted for a day nursery on a busy road where it may generate illegal parking. Your local planning officer will advise you prior to submitting an application.

Planning officials may look more favourably on an application if the applicant is resident in the building or at least in the locality. When the nursery is run by a resident of the area it may then be looked upon as a service to the local community. If the nursery is a small development the number of restrictions on the permission might be less than for a larger nursery with a large clientele and staff. The larger or more 'commercial' enterprise is more likely to be viewed purely as a business development rather than a service to the community.

A sessional service (ie less than full day) may be considered more desirable in some residential areas. Sessional day care such as play groups, pre-schools and after-school groups are not as demanding on facilities as day nurseries.

A Planning Application form is available from the Planning Office and this gives details of the documentation which should accompany your application. A good submission will aid the speedy processing of your application. In addition to the specified documentation, you could include a letter to the planning officer covering such points as:

1   Why you think the premises is suitable for use as a day nursery.
2   Indicate, if relevant, that the nursery development is unlikely to infringe on adjoining properties.
3   The need in the area which it will service.
4   The stopping of cars will not constitute a hazard.
5   Details of the service you will be offering, including the number of children to be catered for and the number of staff to be employed.
6   If possible include letters of support from neighbours and parents of children who will be using the nursery, or references from notable people in the area.
7   Some photographs of the exterior and interior of the building may also help.

If there is a strong lobby against your planning application and you have made a good case in favour, temporary permission may be granted for two to five years, after which time an application for retention must be submitted. If there have been no complaints permission may be granted.

Frequently there are objections from people who fear change or who perceive a day nursery as a places where children run around uncontrolled. The planning officer should be unbiased and able to identify genuine objections. It is a good idea to try and anticipate and deal with all possible objections in your submission.

The granting of planning permission may finally depend on a favourable report from such bodies as the Fire Prevention and Health Authorities. These offices should be contacted prior to submitting your application for planning permission. They may at that stage give you guidelines. When your application is being considered they may be required to submit a report to the Planning Officer. If your application is approved there may be a number of conditions which you will have to fulfil. These conditions could involve, for example, changes to the nursery layout, a restriction on the number of children you may have in the building, payment of service charges etc.

You generally have to pay rates on business premises, based on the rateable valuation of the property. Your local authority will advise you on your liability to pay rates.

There is generally an amount of goodwill within the planning department. Do not be put off by the fear of being refused planning permission. You will have to have permission in order to operate within the law. If you are refused planning permission you may be able to contest the refusal but this usually has to be done within a specified period. Again check with your Planning Authority.

If you have a mortgage on your building and have received permission for a change of use, you may be obliged to inform the bank or building society. The mortgage repayments may be increased from the domestic rate to the usually higher commercial rate.

If you subsequently wish to sell your premises you may be liable for Capital Gains Tax. A solicitor will advise you on whether it would be advisable to offer the property for sale with the change of use or to apply for permission to change back to the original use.

The Workplace Nursery

Many companies are becoming aware of the need to provide child care facilities for the benefit of their employees. The company also has a great deal to gain by providing a workplace nursery, for instance the facility may help the company to retain trained personnel who otherwise would be forced to leave after the birth of a child, and it may also help to attract qualified, experienced staff.

The lack of child care facilities can be an acute problem, especially in rural areas. In the towns and cities there are various options available to working parents, for example child-minders, home helps and so on - provided they can afford them. Rural areas, though, are less likely to have these facilities and may have an even greater need for workplace nurseries. Industries such as light engineering or computer and chemical manufacturing are often encouraged by tax incentives and grants to set up in remote areas where there is rarely a large pool of trained staff in the locality. Thus it may be important for companies such as these to retain their staff. The decision to provide a workplace nursery is unlikely to be made by management alone. The decision is more usually made as a result of negotiations between management, staff and trade unions and specifically at the instigation of women staff.

Workplace nurseries differ from others in three main ways:

* The premises may be supplied by the main sponsor or funded

proportionately by the sponsors.

* The nursery may be situated within the building or grounds of the principle sponsor. It may not be possible to facilitate a nursery on an industrial estate so it may be located off-site but convenient to all involved. As it is usually difficult to find suitable premises, some co-operation from a firm can be a great advantage.

* The management of the nursery may have an element of worker involvement. The principle sponsor may decide that it will be involved in selecting or supplying the premises, but that there its input will end. Alternatively, the sponsor may require that the centre be run by a board of management including a member of their staff and/or parents. This can be an advantage in that there is a certain amount of shared responsibility and decision making. Some nursery managers would, on the other hand, regret this loss of autonomy.

To summarise:

* Workplace nurseries are usually more in demand in an industry where a large proportion of the staff are women with young children.
* Trained staff are expensive to replace and retrain.
* Companies could save in staff costs and dissatisfaction by ensuring reliable child care arrangements are available to staff.
* Companies can be involved to a greater or lesser extent in supplying premises.
* Management will usually be less independent than an owner-run operation.
* Fees may be determined by and/or paid by the company or companies involved.

Chapter Three
Young Children

Children are characterised by their dissimilarity to adults. And this is never more pronounced than in the early years. Most adults live in the world in a state of detached disinterest, rarely overcome with the wonder of life and nature - unlike children.

Newborn children are indeed helpless, with little interest apart from satisfying their bodily requirements. However, they quickly start investigating and exploring: they want first to crawl then to toddle into every corner of the nursery. They are consumed with a desire to find out about themselves and their environment. They want to explore but still need to be able to return to a reassuring hug if something unexpected should be discovered. At this stage, most experiences are new and unfamiliar and children need someone they can relate to and who will nurture their curiosity. Children's natural curiosity can be stunted in a monotonous environment where questions are discouraged and experimenting is considered naughtiness. It is important that there should be neither too many staff changes nor too many staff for young children to interact with.

Young children are also very sensitive to order and disorder. They can become anxious or insecure if they do not have a routine. But while the day should have some order it does not need to be strictly regimented. There should be room for some flexibility within the timetable.

Young children love to imitate the adults around them, their temperament, language and lovingness. Carers must bear in mind their important position in the life of the children, remembering that:

* The first two years of life affect all the rest.
* The baby has great mental powers to which little attention has so far been given.
* Children and babies are supremely sensitive and for that reason any kind of violence produces not only an immediate reaction but may cause permanent problems.

The carer has a duty to help the children's development. She can do this by first looking to the children's environment. Once the environment is physically suitable, in other words if it is safe, clean, bright, orderly and stimulating, then she can concentrate her abilities on needs of a greater complexity:

* Children need love and security,
* They need encouragement and recognition,
* They need new experiences of play and language,
* They need responsibility.

The Environment for Young Children

The carer cannot just 'supply' all that she feels the children need and then simply walk away and let the children 'get on with it'. Time spent with the children is of the utmost importance. They must not be merely supplied with toys and books and left to 'play'. Children's joy does not just come from the books themselves, but also from the pleasure of being held in loving arms and having the books read to them.

Nursery benefits for young children

The benefits of early education in the development of children's full potential deserve to be more widely acknowledged. The nursery environment is planned primarily to facilitate the children and prepared and adapted to their needs. It is in this environment that the children can develop self-confidence and self-determination and have the opportunity to acquire social skills.

One of the earliest benefits of a planned environment is that children are encouraged to make decisions and choices for themselves:

* By choosing their own activities: free choice.
* By planning the order in which they will do their activities: project planning.
* Completing the activity: sense training.
* By tidying up after themselves: developing independence.

Developing skills

In these ways the children develop the social awareness and responsibility so necessary in later life. But in order to develop skills the children must practice and be permitted to learn by trial and error. In order for children to perfect a complex action they must first perfect each component part of that action. By involving the children, the carer helps them to acquire and perfect the basic abilities which will be the building blocks of later skills.

Older children use abilities, perfected by practice, in solving a problem. They will study the problem and then use the appropriate skills required to most effectively resolve it. It is at the experimenting and experiencing stage that children can be thwarted in their efforts. The children's ability to learn new skills can be hindered by the over-zealous carer who is inclined to 'help' children rather than wait patiently as they learn by trial and error.

Let us examine a real life scenario of a child who is given a drink. Often the drink is handed to the child in a covered beaker with a drinking lip. If, later on, the child wants to get a drink for herself, she has not acquired the basic skills to do so:

1   She does not know where to get the drink, as it is always in the beaker.
2   She could not recognise it if she did see it, as it has been hidden in the closed beaker.
3   She could not successfully get it from the jug to the beaker.
4   She may not even have developed the ability to drink it if it was in an uncovered beaker.

This is a small but telling example of what can happen if children are not given the opportunity to practice first one skill then another so that they are finally able to independently choose, pour and drink when they need to. And so it is with all the skills which children must acquire if they are to be fully competent. If the carer continually puts the children's coats on them and closes the buttons they will not have the opportunity to absorb the mechanics of dressing and undressing.

Developing independence

In the same way many children are hindered in their quest for independence in other functions. The nursery is often protected from the children's inclination to 'mess'. Many carers believe that it is their function to serve the children and help them by doing things for them. Children who are served by adults will be totally dependent on them and unable to follow the path to independence. The work of the carer does not consist in serving the children, but in helping them in their self development.

Encouraging security and confidence

It is very important to involve the children in nursery tasks. The familiarity of the objects themselves contributes to the children's sense of security and confidence. The nursery tasks help the children to develop into well-adjusted, competent adults. Involving the children in everyday tasks must be for the sake of working through the processes, rather than for the sake of their immediate results. The more complex activities are best presented in stages. The ability to pour a drink from a large jug to a small glass should be broken into its component skills and each presented and perfected as a step to the final ability. Children should start by carrying the tray, then practice carrying the tray with objects on it, and then pouring liquids between equal sized containers, gradually working their way to the final complex task of pouring without misjudging the amount required. If the children were free to attempt the final exercise without first perfecting the required component abilities they would soon become discouraged by the spills and breakages and frustrated by their failure to get the drink. They would resort to the belief that it is better to let an adult get the drink for them.

The carer is not only concerned with the abilities and everyday skills which the child must acquire. Even without specific opportunities to practice, a child will learn most basic skills with some degree of proficiency. But the character of the child is also developed by these exercises. As Maria Montessori explained:

> The final object of such exercises is the perfecting of the individual who performs them ... A child who has become master of his acts through long and repeated exercises, and who has been encouraged by the pleasant and interesting activities in which he has been engaged, is a child filled with heart and joy and remarkable for his calm and discipline.
>
> *The Discovery of the Child*

There are many excellent books on the developmental stages of the child. It is important that all staff have a good idea of the typical ranges of child development. This is necessary so that the staff can give the children challenges appropriate to their individual developmental stage. It is also important for staff to be able to identify inappropriate behaviour so that remedial help can be sought as soon as possible. (*See Recommended Reading*).

Chapter Four
Why Do Children Misbehave?

Children, like most humans, have a basic wish to belong and be accepted. They want to be accepted first by their mothers, then by their family group and finally by outside groups. In order to belong, children will engage in behaviour which is acceptable to the group to which they strive to belong and they will try, by their behaviour, to be identified with this group.

Very young children can sense disapproval even before they can understand speech. Non-verbal communication such as a frown or a smile from a parent or carer can be a very potent means of changing a child's behaviour. A child will try to avoid disapproval by avoiding the behaviour which elicits this response and will try to gain approval.

Why then do children not behave exactly as their parents want all the time? Perhaps it is better to ask what have children to gain from misbehaviour? The answer, strangely enough, is that children frequently have more to gain by misbehaving than by conforming.

Rudolf Dreikurs, a prominent psychiatrist, categorises children's misbehaviour on the basis of four 'goals' or advantages:

* The first of these goals is **attention**. While children do prefer to gain attention in positive ways, if that fails they will resort to misbehaviour. (Although the attention for misbehaviour is normally negative or punitive, from children's point of view negative attention is preferable to being ignored.) Have you ever noticed how a well-behaved child in a group is frequently left to get on with their play with little or no input from the adults around? Naughty children, on the other hand, are constantly being coaxed, reminded, threatened and finally praised when they do what they were supposed to do to start with. These children can be very quick to misbehave again. They can be very annoying and disruptive in a group but no one can accuse them of failing to get attention!

  To help these attention seeking children we must learn not to 'feed into' their behaviour. We must try to give them positive attention, to focus on their constructive behaviour and ignore their misbehaviour. We must not make them the centre of attention when they misbehave but neither should we go overboard when they behave as they should, as this can cause them to seek praise exclusively. They will receive no satisfaction in attempting anything for themselves and will consider praise as their sole motivation. These children can lack self-motivation and responsibility.

If a child is behaving badly and causing disruption in the group it may not be possible to ignore the misbehaviour. The carer may quietly and without fuss remove such children from the group activity to work on their own with a toy or activity which they cannot break or tear. Children should never be removed from the room and left unsupervised. Neither should they be made to sit in the corner or on the 'bold chair'. This type of punishment may stop the misbehaviour but only in order to avoid further humiliation and not by the child's own choice. While some parents do smack their children (though this should not be encouraged) this should never be the practise in the nursery.

* The second goal is power. Children seeking power can be defiant and have an 'I dare you to make me' look. They may have been forced in the past to behave and now are ready to put up a fight. Their stubbornness can evoke a very strong response in adults. They can defy adults into becoming very vexed, which ultimately only results in an even more heated power struggle. It is important not to become irritated and cross. If the child becomes involved in a power struggle then the child's need to be boss will increase. Just remain calm but firm. Do not try to make children do something just because you are bigger than them. Making a child say 'sorry' or pick up something just because they are afraid of you will only cause the child to become frustrated. Their smallness in the world will be emphasized. Children should be given the opportunity to be in control and to make decisions, such as being given a choice at snack time. If a child consistently wants to control a situation it should be explained that it is not her/his turn and that, while you recognise the disappointment, s/he will have to wait in turn. The child's wish to be in control should be channelled into constructive situations such as helping you or other children.

* If you subdue children by your own superior power they may resort to revenge because they feel very inadequate and frustrated. They feel their pride has been hurt and want to get their own back. They may attempt to verbally abuse the carer either with bad language or by embarrassing one member of

staff in front of another. They may go to another member of staff and say, being sure you are within hearing distance, 'I don't like her, I love you best'. Whatever the emotional response you feel, you must remain calm and continue to show love and affection towards such children. You must be careful not to get into a game of tit-for-tat. It is reassuring to young children that no harm has been done and that your love for them is strong enough to forgive what is, after all, their childishness.

If you are hurt by a child who is old enough to understand, by all means tell the child how you are feeling but do not insist on an apology or you may well end up in another power struggle. The child will learn that adults have feelings too.

Children, like adults, can feel disappointment and anger. Their feelings should be acknowledged and they must not be forced to deny them. Do not say to a child 'big boys and girls don't cry'. Better to let children cry and if necessary let them be angry with you but hug them while they take this opportunity to 'liquidate' their feelings. Do not try simply to get children to stop crying but rather comfort them so that they can stop crying when they feel better. Children who are not permitted to cry will seek every opportunity to cause tears, even to the point of antagonising another child to provoke a fight.

* The fourth goal described by Dreikurs is **display of inadequacy**. This occurs when children are very despondent and have given up the fight. They have been defeated and forced to comply by adults' superior strength. These children have lost their spirit and will respond passively or even cower. Their discouragement leads to a very poor self image. The catch phrase of these children is "I can't". It is most important that they are not criticised. Their qualities and strengths must be highlighted and continuously focused on. They must be permitted to help and encouraged to do things for themselves. The environment needs thoughtful planning so they will be able to solve their problems and begin to feel secure and confident in the world. They should be encouraged carry out creative activities such as sand and water play, using play dough, etc. Allow them time to put on their own coats. Encourage their parents to dress them in clothes which the children can manage by themselves when going to the toilet.

Be aware of the way you speak to the children. Try to replace commands, such as *don't*, *hurry*, *stop* or *wait* with explanations, such as *if you kick me I will be sad as it hurts me* or *if you do not tidy away you will be late for break and miss 'newstime'.*

Although I have presented the goals of misbehaviour as a cycle within the carer/child relationship, it is quite possible that certain children will have acquired their misbehaving traits before entering the nursery. The parent/child relationship is more complex than that of the carer with the child. Nonetheless the carer/child relationship is important and can effect a child's self esteem. A child who is experiencing a poor relationship with her/his parents can, with your encouragement, build up feelings of self worth which s/he would otherwise not have the opportunity to do. Conversely you can damage a child's self image by being insensitive to the needs of the individual child.

Encouragement

One of the most important methods of improving a child's feeling of self worth and confidence is through encouragement. Encouragement, often mistaken for praise, is the process whereby the carer focuses on the child's assets and strengths instead of focussing on the child's mistakes. Society has encouraged adults to become expert at finding fault, to expect the worst, and in general to be discouraging towards our children. Maria Montessori saw the dangers of both praise and criticism: "There is one thing she (the carer) must never do and that is to interfere by praising a child's work, or punishing him if it is wrong, even by correcting his mistakes."

At the time she wrote this was a very radical notion but now psychologists are discovering the importance of neither focussing on mistakes nor praising. It should be remembered that children cannot improve unless they feel good about themselves and believe they have the ability to improve. There is an inherent danger in using a child's self-concept to get them to do good work. We frequently tell children how clever they are when they do things correctly, but if they do not complete the exercise correctly then clearly they may assume that they are not good or clever.

Praise can be discouraging. It is a type of reward. It is based on winning and being best. In effect, the carer who praises is indicating to the child that, because the child has done something the carer considers worthwhile, the child will have the reward of being recognised and valued by the carer instead of being recognised and valued just for themselves. Praise is an attempt to motivate children with external rewards. Like punishment it is a method of controlling the group. The children who conform to the standards set by the carer will be successful in earning praise. They may make decisions which are not in their own interests in order to gain praise, for example they might eat a dinner they detest because 'a good girl finishes her dinner'.

Praise, or the absence of it, will discourage children in the same way as punishment.

> If children worry so much about failure, might it not be because they rate success too high and depend on it too much? May there not be altogether too much praise for good work in the lower grades? If, when Johnny does good work, we make him feel 'good', may we not, without intending it, be making him feel 'bad' when he does bad work?
> John Holt *How Children Fail*.

If a child is observed doing an activity, for example a jigsaw, incorrectly the common response is to intervene. The carer may go to the child and perhaps take the jigsaw, saying kindly "you are doing it wrong, here, let me show you how to do it right". If the child continues to do it incorrectly the carer may say something like "Look! I'll show you one more time, if you can't do it I'll have to put it away." If the child continues to be unable to do the exercise the carer may say "you can't do it, try something easier" and put the exercise away. If the child's inabilities and failures are focused on to this extent, the child can only conclude that s/he has only failings and is worthless in the eyes of the carer. This is negative reinforcement even though the carer was kind and will no doubt 'praise' the child when s/he finds something which is easy enough to do.

The carer must learn to separate the deed from the doer. Children will not always perform as we would like. We must let them know that they are valued as persons no matter how they perform. Instead of focussing on the element of an exercise the child has done incorrectly, the carer should encourage the child to focus on those aspects that were correctly done or enjoyed. At the same time, make a mental note that this exercise will need to be re-explained to the child. For children it is the doing of the exercise rather than the accomplishment of the task which gives most pleasure.

If we want children to see themselves as worthwhile persons, we must genuinely accept them as they are, with all their imperfections, and not just as we would wish them to be. In this way we will help them to accept themselves. It is important for both children and adults to realise that it is normal to make mistakes. This should not be explained in a way that implies that the person is less worthy on account of their mistakes. Nor should it be implied that, while mistakes are normal, they are an indication of inability. By being separated from any degree of blame in making mistakes, children, and also adults, will be able to admit their mistakes without losing face or respect. Both the carer and child must learn to accept themselves and one another. The carer must not hold herself up as all-powerful in front of the children. Neither must she expect too much from them. Children do not have the maturity to control their reactions but nevertheless the carer must respect them enough to listen to them and discuss rather than command.

Understanding yourself can be as important as understanding the children in your care. The nursery manager should have a degree of 'self-knowledge'.

Ten Child Care Commandments

1 Give continuous, consistent, loving care - it's as essential for mental health as food is for the body.

2 Give generously of your time and understanding - playing with and reading to the children matters more than a tidy, smooth running play room.

3 Provide new experiences and bathe the children in language - this enriches their growing minds.

4 Encourage children to play in every way both alone and with other children - exploring, imitating, constructing, pretending and creating.

5 Give more recognition of effort than achievement.

6 Give children ever-increasing responsibility - like all skills responsibility needs to be practised.

7 Remember that every child is unique - what is suitable handling for one may not be suitable for another.

8 Make the way you show your disapproval fit the individual child's temperament, age and understanding.

9 Never threaten that you will stop loving a child or give her or him away; you may reject the behaviour but never suggest that you will reject the child.

10 Do not expect gratitude. The child is with you not by her own choice but by the choice of others.

Adapted from: Mia Kellmer Pringle *The Needs of Children*.

Chapter Five
Play and Equipment

Play, according to Maria Montessori, is the work of the child. It is this and more! It is children's way of developing and perfecting skills, it is the integrating force of all early learning. It is a means of discovering and exploring both the world and the self. When children play, they develop control and coordination of their bodies through movement. They also experiment with emotions. In a play situation, children can find an outlet for their emotions and learn the means of coping with them.

> Play can be defined as behaviour that is intrinsically
> motivated, freely chosen, process-orientated and
> pleasurable.
> *Johnson and Ershler*

It is vital that people charged with helping children to develop to their full potential understand the importance of play in children's lives and that sufficient time and staff are devoted to a variety of play opportunities. To facilitate play as defined by Johnson and Ershler, a number of play opportunities must be presented in a well planned environment. Children must be neither limited to organised group play activities nor to continuous, unplanned freeplay.

While playing, children combine elements of imagination, adventure, creation, coordination and manipulation. Toys and play materials stimulate their curiosity and aid their emotional, cognitive and physical development. Growing mastery over materials also gives them reassurance and satisfaction. While some rules are essential for the smooth running of the nursery, remember that the nursery is *home* to the children and should not be too restricting, regimented or institutional. The carer's greatest contribution to the children's development is a warm and happy relationship with them. The more the carer enjoys being with the children and doing things with them, the more the children will enjoy their achievements.

Group Activities

Advance preparation is necessary for organised play and group activities. Children can lose interest very quickly if they have to wait while you hunt for the glue or glitter! Select activities according to the abilities of the children and also their mood. You may have prepared an indoor activity on a day when the weather turns out unusually good, be prepared to be flexible. Try to organise an activity so that children of varying ability can enjoy the activity at their own level. Give the children choices and the opportunity to participate in planning for activities. The children often find more satisfaction in the doing rather than the result. Remember to encourage the children by acknowledging their efforts rather than the end result. Use the opportunity to speak with them in a constructive way, for example a question like "would you like to tell me about what you have made?" has more scope for dialogue than "what's that?"

It is important to remember that children's play passes through a series of developmental stages. Piaget described the earliest play between children as parallel play. While the children may be using the same materials or toys, each is working independently. At about the age of three we begin to see cooperative play, in which two or more children join in the same activity. At about this age children begin to have 'best friends'. At all stages children will need opportunities for solitary play.

While facilitating solitary, parallel and cooperative play the range of activities should always aim to:

1   Develop the interpersonal skills of the children through group interaction.
2   Develop their learning experiences and means of communicating.
3   Stimulate the creative impetus, imagination and awareness level of the children.
4   Promote the social development of the children through organised play and structured learning experiences.
5   Encourage freedom of speech. Time should be taken to listen to each child.
6   Include developmental activities to promote gross and fine motor movements and hand-eye coordination.

A consistent, coordinated, caring approach to play activities is recommended. Play must not become a burden to either the children or the staff.

Equipment

An environment planned for totally safe play would be quite restrictive. Some equipment and materials have a certain element of 'danger', for example sand can be thrown into children's eyes, and children can fall from even the smallest slide. The play equipment must present the children with a challenge and be satisfying to use. Instructing the children in the correct use of equipment combined with constant supervision of play can eliminate the chance of accidents while giving the children scope to develop.

Toys are the tools of children's development. While choosing and shopping for equipment can be very enjoyable, it is also a serious task. Not only must you look for value for money, you also need to choose toys which fulfil the many and varied needs of your children. Good quality toys may be more expensive but they tend to be safer and will last longer so they are less expensive in the long run. The use of inexpensive domestic articles and discarded items such as large boxes will meet many of their play needs. (See *Appendix V*).

It may not be necessary to acquire all the equipment before opening your nursery but it should be budgeted for in the long term. Some second-hand furniture can be purchased through newspapers. There should be low, fixed shelving from which children can easily choose and replace toys. Toy storage units which will be used as area dividers should be low and broad. Large toy boxes can be used but they must not be too deep as a child may fall into them.

The following is a list of the types of equipment a day nursery may need.

Large Equipment

* Climbing frame and slide (indoor or out)
* Seesaw
* Large construction system such as Quadro
* Baby Walker
* Tricycles
* Rocking horse
* Nursery trampoline
* Water play table
* Sand pit
* Sand/Water toys: funnels, spades, buckets etc.

Early Learning

* Activity centre
* Mobiles
* Stacking toys
* Posting toys
* Threading, lacing toys
* Train, car track
* Classification, sorting, matching toys
* Books
* Jigsaws
* Easy grip board jigsaws
* Inset boards, Size grading boards, Floor jigsaws
* Interlocking toys

Imaginative Play

* Dressing-up clothes
* Puppets, Dolls
* Play house area
* Farm/zoo animals
* Cooker, sink, cooking set
* Tea set

Construction Toys

* Varied range of construction toys for the different age ranges of children.

Arts and Crafts

* Paints, brushes, pots, crayons etc.
* Paper, glue
* Play dough
* Children's scissors (left and right handed)

Musical Instruments

* Bells
* Cymbals
* Drums
* Maraccas

Furniture

* Book cases
* Storage crates
* Chairs, tables
* Boxes
* Cots

The Play Space

When planning a play environment the following categories of play need to be considered:

* Creative and 'Messy' Play
  eg Water, sand, painting, pencils, crayons, clay, play-dough.

* Imaginative Play
  eg Dressing up-clothes, home corner, dolls' houses, cots, prams, puppets, cars, garages, farm, train, boats

* Exercises for fine motor movement
  eg Jigsaws, filling and grading toys, matching games, pegs and pegboards, large beads, straws, lego, wooden blocks (dyed not painted), children's scissors.

* Exercises for gross motor development
  eg Slide, climbing frame, swings, tricycles, bicycles, outdoor and adventure play. *Note safety.*

* Language development and speech exercises
  eg Good quality story books, picture books, story telling, news and conversation time, rhymes, word games, songs.

* For Younger Children
  eg Rattles, soft toys, teething rings, push-and-pull toys, posting boxes, pop-up toys, hammer and pegs, rag dolls.

Creative Play

Playing with water is a most enjoyable activity for children whether in groups or individually. Children love water, it drips, it splashes, it pours and it sparkles! They can discover the properties of water by experimenting with a variety of containers, funnels, pumps and sponges, objects which float or sink. Water can be very soothing for unsettled or aggressive children.

The first rule of water play is *prepare the area*. Outdoor water play is best but is dependent on the weather. For indoor water play, a carpeted area is less desirable but if necessary the carpet can be protected with a plastic sheet. Cover a hard floor with large towels to prevent the children slipping. A child-sized mop should be supplied and the children can be encouraged to be involved in cleaning up. Whether indoors or out, unless the weather is very warm the children should be well protected with waterproof apron and sleeves. A shallow baby bath or a basin on a table can be used in place of a custom-made water-play table. The number of children around the water-play table should be limited so that each child has a reasonable area of water and a choice of objects. Too many children can lead to disorder and fighting.

Sand is even more versatile than water. Children love to feel fine dry sand running through their fingers. Dry sand is clean and pours and can give the children satisfaction from pouring and sieving exercises. For the wet sand they will need containers to mould castles etc. Digging and cars are synonymous with sand. Separate plastic cars and construction vehicles should be kept for use in the sand pit to prevent sand spreading to other areas.

As with water play, the children and the floor should be protected for playing with sand. Brushing up sand is an excellent exercise which the children will enjoy all the more if the brush and dustpan are child-sized. Outdoor sand-pits must be covered when not in use to prevent fouling by animals.

Playdough is a perennial favourite with both children and adults. It can be satisfying for the children to pound, pull, shape and roll. Only after much experiment with the playdough on its own should you introduce tools and equipment such as rolling pins, plastic knives, blunt scissors etc. Children can make shapes with pastry cutters which can be allowed to dry and then painted. Playdough should be stored in an airtight container in the fridge. It should not be kept for too long as it will go off.

While bought playdough comes in a variety of colours and lasts very well, buying it denies the children the fun of making it!

Playdough recipe

> 4 cups flour
> 1 cup salt
> food colouring in a dropper bottle
> $1/2$ cup cooking oil
> enough water to make dough pliable but not sticky

Mix together flour, salt, oil and two or three drops of colouring. Add water slowly until required consistency is reached. Knead well.

The making of playdough gives opportunities for;

* Counting (cups of flour)
* Comparing (flour and salt ... they look the same, do they feel the same? Do they taste the same?)

* Mixing (Colouring in water, colouring in oil, oil and water, water and flour).

For painting and drawing you will require copious quantities of paper. Children from an early age have a great love of scribbling and so drawing equipment should be supplied for all ages. The young children will need large stubby crayons while the older children may prefer finer colouring pencils and pens. If it is not possible to give the children unlimited access to drawing and painting materials a large blackboard and chalk should be provided.

Painting should be in an area reserved especially for the purpose. This area should have a washable floor and facilities for hand-washing. Short thick brushes and ready-mix paints are generally preferred by children and spill-proof paint-pots are desirable. The children's clothes must be well protected, as otherwise a relaxing exercise can become nerve-racking for both children and staff if they have to be constantly careful of their clothes and the floor.

Variations of painting include finger painting, foot painting, bubble painting, blob pictures - the possibilities are endless.

Imaginative Play

Role play, dressing up and pretend play enables children to explore and act out situations and relationships. Children can experiment with their feelings, fears and anxieties. They can become cross with their teddies and then comfort them. They can become police officers or doctors and be all grown up for just as long as they like, safe in the knowledge that they can go back to being themselves as soon as they have had enough.

The furniture in the home corner should lend itself to being converted from a home to a shop, hospital or whatever, and should have easy access to dressing-up clothes. There should be a variety of props to facilitate different role play, such as a doctor's kit, kitchen equipment, cash register and so on.

Dolls' houses, farms and garages can help children imagine and control situations. The dolls' house should contain furniture and figures and perhaps a car. This equipment should reflect a sensitivity to the true life experiences of the nursery children. When children live in high rise buildings and use public transport, they do not relate to the four-bedroomed detached dolls' house with a garage. All children should have access to a variety of ethnic costumes, dolls, etc. There should be a farm and/or zoo with a good supply appropriate animals.

Exercises for fine motor movement

The children should have free access to toys, games and jigsaws. These activities are particularly useful in helping to develop hand and eye coordination, visual perception and discrimination. Table top toys are a great favourite with the children and have the added bonus of helping to develop concentration and pre-reading skills. Jigsaws must range from the knobbed, two or three piece, fit-in type to the more complex interlocking kind.

Wooden building blocks and other construction toys are extremely versatile and there should be a range of small and large blocks. Blocks provide opportunities for practising and mastering a variety of skills. The children develop coordination while building towers, and patience as they fail. They can use the blocks as cars, boats, dolls' house furniture or other imaginative play. Blocks also lend themselves well to parallel and cooperative play. They challenge the older children to design and plan their own road networks and towns, both alone and in a group. This type of activity provides ample opportunities for co-operation, planning and other social interaction.

Exercises for gross motor development

The children need space in which to run, jump, climb, ride bikes and so on. Ideally they should have an opportunity to play outside for some part of each day, even if it is cool. On cooler days children can be organised to play ball games or chasing. Most days are suitable for some running around outside if the children are appropriately dressed.

A trip to the park or going for a walk is an excellent form of exercise and is an opportunity for children to splash in puddles, kick leaves etc. Walks are not recommended, though, unless there is a sufficient number of adults in attendance. There should be one adult to three children, and the younger children should be kept in pushchairs until they arrive at the park.

Indoor equipment should facilitate dancing, climbing, play tunnelling, trampolines etc. The large play areas should not encroach on areas where other children are playing. (*See Appendix Four: Suggested Layouts*).

Language development

Books or a small library should be in an area reserved for quiet activities. It is important that children have access to books from an early age and books should be part of every child's experience. Board books and washable books can be on the lower shelves for younger children and paper books can be kept on higher shelves for the older ones. Books are a source of entertainment and imagination as well as knowledge and help develop attitudes which will remain with the child.

There is nothing to be gained by reading stories which frighten or upset the children. Books should be chosen with care and should be multi-racial, with non-stereotyped sex roles for the characters. They should not glorify violence or frighten the children.

Group storytelling is generally more suitable for children over three years old, while younger children respond better to one-to-one stories and picture books. Joining a story group should be a privilege rather than a duty for children, they should be there because they want to be there, and they must behave in such a way so as not to spoil the time for other children. The group should be kept small so that all the children can see the storyteller and her book if she is reading the story. The reader should be very familiar with the story so that she can read it upside-down while showing the pictures to the children. Story tapes are also an effective way of relating the story but lack the personal touch, as the children cannot have any input with a tape whereas they can, and do, with a person.

Use the times when children are gathered together, such as before meals or at story time, to encourage them to tell their news. This gives them a chance to learn how to take turns to talk, an important lesson in conversation. It also lets them experience the difference between reality, as in news, and fiction, as in stories. Sometimes newstime develops into a type of story time but the children can be gently drawn back to reality in their news. Group times can also be an opportunity for rhymes, songs and word games. Through rhymes and songs the children develop their sense of rhythm, and word games can develop diction and speaking ability. Even nonsense words have their place in developing vocabulary and speech. (See *Speech and Music.*)

For younger children

The infant is not simply a passive sleeping and feeding machine. Even at birth the newborn infant has an immediate reaction to the environment. The reaction can range from being stunned, fearful and disturbed to feeling quiet, relaxed and peaceful. Most newborns spend the first few hours adjusting physically to the world around them. The bright lights and noise of a hospital are very alien to the infant who has just left the warm, peaceful, gurgling environment of the womb.

Very soon, though, infants begin to adjust to the sounds, sights, smells and feelings around them. Even very young infants can react to and be comforted by the sounds around them. They react to touch especially to touching on their faces and hands. With time they learn to focus on objects further than eight inches away, so mobiles and coloured pictures hold their interest. But human voices and faces are still the most fascinating thing to infants. Rattles and teething rings can be inspected and taste-tested from an early age and when babies are able to sit up, they will enjoy experimenting with rolling, rattling and knocking objects over.

By the time children are beginning to say their first words and take their first tentative steps they will be starting to explore the play area for themselves. The older children can become irritated if the toddlers are given unrestricted access to their games as the babies can spoil their efforts. Older children should have an area where they can construct and play without hindrance, but they should also be given opportunities to mix with toddlers at other times.

The younger children can learn a lot from being in the company of older children, but they can also lose out if they have to compete for toys or attention. The younger children should have their own area within the general play room. This area can be in the form of a very large playpen remembering to allow a minimum of 2.5 square metres of space per child.

Toys in this area should be reserved for the use of the younger children and washed daily. Younger children may not be as able to demand adult attention as the older children, so it is important that an adult remains in this area with the younger children. Pre-walking children can communicate quite effectively and enjoy games such as 'peek-a-boo,' playing with rattles, songs and clapping hands, hiding things under cloths, exploring hands and faces and cuddling.

Though staff will have no doubt learned during their training about the stages of play and will have many ideas for games and activities in the early days, it is all too easy to 'dry up' on ideas occasionally. It is therefore a good idea to have some reference books available to the staff covering both child development and ideas for activities. *See Recommended Reading*.

Chapter Six
Speech and Music

Encouraging the Development of Speech

To maintain a satisfying relationship with their peers and with adults, children must learn how to communicate effectively. To do this they must speak in a manner which can be understood and with a fluency which will enable them to convey their meaning concisely and without ambiguity. They must first learn the mechanisms of speech and then a vocabulary to facilitate communication.

If children are to learn proper speech, then they must hear proper speech in use, be encouraged to speak properly and be listened to patiently so that their efforts to speak are recognised. It frequently happens that children in groups are competing for the attention of the staff. If particular children are reserved or have difficulty expressing themselves, they may find that they are being overwhelmed by the more vocal, boisterous children. The carer must be aware of this and give each child an opportunity to speak and be listened to.

It is important that the carer does not encourage the children to speak in a way that is particular to them and not recognisable to others. While 'baby talk' is an important step in understanding it must not become the language of the nursery. While the nursery carer may understand or encourage baby talk, children will quickly become frustrated and confused when they cannot make themselves understood in the wider world. They will use the only words they know to communicate and will be unable to comprehend why they are being misunderstood. It is most important for the children that the carer be patient with them and pronounce slowly and clearly the words for which they struggle. Though she may understand the children's baby words the carer should encourage the children to make the effort to use the correct word and to say it properly. The ability to name things enables children to refer to them through language rather than gesture.

Books also play a vital role in the development of children's linguistic abilities. Language development, which is so important to children in both the short and long-term, is stimulated and encouraged when they read or have books read to them.

Answering Questions

The children should be encouraged to ask questions:

* Do take their questions seriously and do not laugh at them. Children's questions and the answers they receive are very important in helping them to understand the world and their position in it.
* Children do not always ask the question they seem to be asking. Think about your answer, and consider the context in which the question is asked. The answer to "Where did I come from?" might be on one occasion "Galway" and on another something more complex.
* Do call things by their names. If children have a problem they want to explain to another adult they must have the correct terminology. They can learn the slang terms they might need from their peers.
* Do give honest answers in language which the children can understand.
* Do not give long boring answers or tell them more than they want to know.
* If you do not know the answer to a question, tell the child that you don't know but if possible find out or help them to find out. If the answer is available to the children encourage them to observe and discover for themselves. For instance, if a child is watching a plumber at work and asks "what is she doing?" you can tell the child to watch and see if s/he can discover the answer.

Music in the Nursery Environment

Artistic expression - singing, dancing, playing musical instruments - should be an essential part of child rearing. John Dewey, the American philosopher and educational theorist, argued that because the arts are so distinctly human they are among the highest and most important forms of communication. If one accepts this view, the arts assume a significant role in the nursery. It is very important for children to become aware of a wide range and diversity of traditions, customs and perspectives. Through artistic experiences, children can come to understand something of the lifestyle and patterns of meaning in cultures other than their own.

George Eliot claimed "there is no feeling, except the extremes of fear and grief, that does not find relief in music." For many children, their own emotions can be quite frightening and they can find difficulty in understanding their unpredictable emotional swings. Music, through its expression of emotions, can help children to understand and accept their feelings and emotions. Music is a direct line of communication with the child's spirit. It can be very reassuring for children to hear music which expresses emotions which they recognise.

Perhaps the most readily identifiable emotional image which children can glean from music is happiness. Children who are feeling a bit low will brighten at the sound of a gay tune being played. When the children are restless, playing a happy dancing tune seems to help them become less irritable, even though some of the children may not join in the dance. Singing can pass the time while children wait for a meal to be served, for instance. No amount of coercing and cajoling can accomplish what music does.

Music should be introduced to the children in the nursery as a part of the environment and not as a distinct 'subject'. The children must have the opportunity to hear a mixture of children's songs and rhymes, popular songs and classical music. While the songs and rhymes can be introduced as a group activity music must not be relegated just to set periods. The children should have the opportunity to listen to music, perhaps while they play with play dough etc.

Their first introduction to moving to music will require some discipline, for example, all moving around in one direction, or prompting such as: "this music is danger music". As the children develop self-discipline they should have more freedom to move about the room and interpret the music without too much direction from the adults. In this way the focus will move from the adult to the music.

They should also have the opportunity to move freely while they listen and to march and play musical instruments such as marracas, drums, cymbals etc. This can be a very noisy activity, naturally, and encouraged only when there are no sleeping babies in the nursery!

Chapter Seven
Nature Study in the Nursery

Growing plants or flowers helps the children to realise where living things come from. It also helps them develop a sense of responsibility and demonstrates the difference between things grown for aesthetic purposes and things grown for utilitarian purposes, and shows them the origins of many everyday foods.

Initially it is important to concentrate on fast-growing plants so that the children do not lose interest before anything has happened. Cress is a favourite for children to grow as it grows very quickly on almost any damp surface. It can be grown on damp blotting paper, cotton wool or even, to great effect, in an empty egg shell. The children can help to plant the seeds and the cress is most unlikely to fail. The seeds should be covered with paper or card and stored in a warm place. The nursery is usually suitably warm. Within two or three days the seeds will begin to sprout, much to the delight of the children. The young plants are then placed near the window. The children can 'harvest' and eat the resulting cress plants, though some are too unadventurous to do so!

Plants to grow and eat

* Bean shoots: Ready in a matter of days, may not be very popular to eat but fun to grow.
* Scallions: Ready in about six weeks, an acquired taste.
* Lettuce: Ready in four to six weeks. Will continue to grow if just leaves are taken.
* Beans: Broad, French etc. Can be started in a glass to show roots. Ready in about ten weeks. Some of the harvest may be sown again.
* Peas: Like beans, peas can be started in glass and some of the harvest sown again. Very tasty raw.

Remember that the more you grow the greater the incidence of failure! Do not be discouraged but use these occasions to discuss what went wrong and experiment with new ways of growing.

The children can discuss other growing things which people eat. Then they can discuss the foods that other animals eat. They could put up a bird table in the winter and put out a selection of foods to see which kinds the birds like. The birds' preferences or needs for seeds and berries can also be discussed.

Naturally the theme of food will evolve over a period of weeks or months, so there is no need to inflict vast amounts of information on the children in the space of one day or week. As with all information, children should be given time to think about it.

As the children become accustomed to waiting for things to grow, slower growing things such as pansies and sunflowers can be introduced. It can be interesting to grow their own plant seeds. Peas are an excellent choice for this. The children can grow one or two peas each. A few peas can be grown in a jar of cotton wool to show the root and shoot appearing, though the root may be too delicate to withstand being transplanted into soil. Some seeds can be grown on dry blotting paper to show that they will not thrive. There will no doubt be some failures among the children's plants, the reasons for the failures can be discussed and hopefully not repeated. Of the plants which do flower and bear seeds, some of the resulting peas can be eaten, some fed to the birds, and some planted again for a crop from the children's own seeds. The children can note the original number of seeds planted, the number of seeds obtained from the first crop and the seeds from the second crop. Many different plants can be planted, some for food, some for flowers and some, such as the sunflower, for the flower, the food and the sheer wonder of its height.

An outing into the country, if possible, is both exciting and informative for city-bred children. It will help children to understand both the beauty and the value of the natural world, and our responsibility to conserve and protect it.

Chapter Eight
Food and Nutrition

Developing Good Food Habits and Attitudes

One of our basic needs, food serves three general functions:

1 Food supplies energy.
2 Food supplies essential nutrients for growth and development.
3 Mealtimes provide pleasure and time for interaction.

Consider when we invite guests to a meal. We do not intend just to feed them and then send them on their way. The meal is a sharing experience and the trouble we go to indicates the esteem in which we hold our guests. Advertising agencies have identified the importance of food in the mother-child relationship. In marketing their food, they do not just concentrate on its nutritional value, they often use images of sharing food as a symbol of love and intimacy.

Mealtime is a very important time. In the home it is an opportunity for the family to get together and share their experiences of the day. In the nursery, too, the child can see mealtime as a time to enjoy, not just the food, but also the social interaction. Mealtime can be a time for practicing new skills, practical as well as social.

The day nursery can offer opportunities for the children to become involved in planning, buying, preparing and serving meals.

Planning

The children can read stories which contain fruit and vegetables, for instance *Green Eggs and Ham* by Dr Seuze, *Winnie the Pooh and Some Bees* by AA Milne and *The Enormous Turnip* to name but a few.

The children can discuss the different ways various foods can be prepared. They can help prepare a lunch such as vegetable soup. Each child can bring in one vegetable for the soup. Many vegetables will not need to be peeled but just washed thoroughly by the children and then diced by the adult. The children can even grow and eat their own vegetables in the nursery garden. If space is limited a window box will do.

Food should be inviting, colourful and easy to eat. Young children will get exasperated with food which is continually falling off the spoon. Instead of serving spaghetti, try pasta shells or spirals. Spaghetti, without sauce, can be served and will no doubt turn into a game of sucking up snakes! Finger food is more inviting than soggy cooked vegetables. A good rule of thumb is - if you would not eat it, why expect a child to?

Children should be given five to ten minutes advance notice of mealtime to give them time to finish their game and tidy up. Mealtimes should not intrude on other activities without warning, as this can make the children very irritated at the prospect of having to eat and may result in their developing a negative attitude to food.

Tables and chairs should be child-sized and infants should be accommodated at the table if at all possible. Ideally children should eat in 'family groups', in other words groups which include children of mixed ages and abilities and an adult. The groups should be as small as the number of adults will permit. There are several advantages to having both the children and the adults eating together, it enables the adults to conduct newstime or other activities, and the fact that the adults have a vested interest in the meals will encourage a varied and interesting menu. The main benefit stems from the interaction of the children with each other and with the adult. Mealtime in the nursery should be a 'family' rather than a 'canteen' experience.

Once they have arrived at the table the children should not have to wait too long before being served. They can become restless and conflicts may arise between the children or with the adults.

When the meal arrives, it is better if the children are not simply presented with a plate with the food already on it. Some of the older children should be assigned to set the table, and possibly bring the slightly cooled food to the table in serving dishes. The adults or older children can then ask each child individually what they would like - "would you like some carrots/chicken/peas?". The child may answer "yes please" or "no thank you" and their choices should be respected. In this way the children learn the names of the foods and will also be making their own choices. Older children may like to serve themselves.

The children should each be given less food than they are likely to eat and told to ask for more if they want it. The children will learn table manners and become familiar with the tableware. By helping the children to develop a good attitude to mealtimes, the nursery is giving them the freedom to develop.

Mealtimes should be enjoyable so conflicts should be avoided. Children and adults are equally capable of using food to manipulate - children may learn to refuse food in order to provoke a particular response from adults, while adults may deny children certain types of food, such as dessert, as a form of punishment. Children, like adults, have likes and dislikes. Their right to make choices should be respected and adults should not try to force a child to eat. If the finishing of food becomes a big issue the adults may turn mealtime into an opportunity for conflict. If the food is unfamiliar to a child, s/he can be encouraged to take just a little on her/his plate and try it if s/he wants to. Children are more likely to try strange foods if they know they will not be forced to finish them.

With a little thought, meals can be both nutritious and interesting. it is important for the children to have a balanced diet but not necessary for them to get their nutritional requirements from the same food source every day. For example:

Sources of protein

1 oz meat
1 egg
1 oz cheese
$1/_4$ cup cottage cheese
$1/_2$ cup dried peas or beans
2 tablespoons peanut butter

Sources of calcium

1 cup of milk
1 cup yoghurt
$1^1/_4$ cup cottage cheese
$1^1/_2$ cup ice cream
$1^3/_4$ oz cheese

See Appendix One: Healthy Eating Every Day.

Figure 1: Foods to avoid and foods to encourage

Avoid	Encourage

Snacks
* Salty foods, crisps, nuts
* Sweet foods, cakes, biscuits, sweets
* Sweet drinks, squashes

Meals
* Sausages, bacon
* Meat pies, pasties
* Fruit canned in syrup
* Suet puddings, sweet custard
* Cream, synthetic instant whips

Cooking
* Peeling edible skin
* Long boiling, frying or roasting

Snacks
* Wholegrain bread, rolls, pitta
* Smooth peanut butter [1]
* Fresh & dried fruit
* Plain popcorn [2]
* Pure fruit juices diluted

Meals
* Freshly made homemade soup
* Pasta, rice, beans, pulses
* Plain boiled potatoes [3]
* Raw or lightly cooked vegetables
* Fish, lean meat
* Fruit tarts or crumble made with wholemeal flour and unsaturated fat
* Homemade natural yogurt with fresh puree fruit added

Cooking
* Prepare vegetables just before using
* Light boiling, poaching
* Steaming, stir frying, baking

[1] *Do not give young children chunky peanut butter or nuts.*
[2] *Do not add salt, butter or sugar glaze.*
[3] *Do not add salt or butter.*

Children can be involved in both food and mealtime preparation, helping them to develop skills and important concepts. For example, concepts which can be experienced while experimenting with food are:

* Colour: The different colours of fruits and vegetables. The different shades of colour eg green lettuce, green cabbage. Food may change colour in cooking.
* Hand-eye coordination: Pouring liquids, making up squash, eg 1 part juice to 4 parts water.
* Vocabulary: Hot, cold, warm, bitter, sweet, enough, more, less, etc.
* Sorting and matching: Sorting cutlery and dishes, sorting and putting away canned food.
* Freezing and thawing: Water to ice and ice to water. Making Ice-pops.

Food Costs Money

Children, like Napoleon's army, march on their stomachs. Healthy physical development is a prerequisite if children are to benefit positively from their environment. Why is it then that some nurseries spend a lot of money on equipment yet still rely heavily on convenience and processed foods to see their children through the long nursery day? Changing towards a better diet which includes more fresh ingredients will benefit the children's health. It can also save money and make mealtimes more interesting for staff and children alike.

It is more challenging and enjoyable for staff to plan and prepare an interesting menu rather than just repetitively 'warm up' pre-packaged food. It is unlikely that the total time required in preparing fresh food will be much more than that needed for preparing processed food. Admittedly it is quicker to open a can of spaghetti than to boil fresh pasta but the minimal increase in time spent in preparation is offset by the savings in costs. Fresh produce is usually cheaper than its processed counterpart, except for produce such as fruit. Fruit out of season is more expensive than canned. Most canned fruit contains syrup, although you can now get fruit tinned in its own juice, with no added sugar. There is usually enough fruit available all year round to ensure that the nursery has a cheap and plentiful supply. Fruit can be prepared in the nursery and kept frozen until required.

Savings in costs will also result from healthier cooking - stir frying or serving food raw is cheaper than roasting or boiling. Because fresh food is more interesting, it's likely that there will be less wasted so in the long run, it works out less expensive. The image of wholesome food as being more expensive is a fallacy. Because whole foods have tended to be sold in specialist and expensive health food shops, they are still considered luxury items. Nothing could be further from the truth. Processed foods are expensive to produce and are heavily marketed, it is only logical that these added costs will be borne by the consumer.

Breastfeeding mothers should be encouraged to try to continue breastfeeding for as long as they feel comfortable doing so. It may be possible for the mother to come to the nursery on her lunch break and during the evening. The nursery staff can bottlefeed the baby if s/he is hungry between feeds. The mother can supply expressed milk or formula in a bottle each morning for this purpose. Babies whose feeds are being mixed in this way may prefer a bottle with a teat which is shaped like a human breast such as 'Even Flo' and 'Avent'. Some babies can be so regular in their demands to be fed that their mothers, especially those who are self-employed or working on flexitime, can feed them before work, during lunch breaks and before leaving the nursery in the evening.

The nursery should have a good cookery book for the use of staff and also a cookery book designed specifically for children so that they can become involved in menu planning. *See Recommended Reading*.

Sample menus

Select one breakfast, mid day snack, lunch and afternoon snack per day.

Breakfast

Cereal chosen for its nutritional and fibre content, eg:
* Weetabix
* Bran
* Shredded Wheat
* Porridge.

Mid day snack

* Fruit juice with a plain biscuit, cracker or rusk.

Lunch

* Welsh Rarebit, salad and potatoes, milk.
* Shepherd's pie with cheese, carrots, milk.
* Stir fry vegetables, rice or noodles, milk.
* Vegetable and lentil soup, brown bread toasted, milk.

* Fish Fingers, white sauce (made from strong flour), raw vegetable fingers, milk.

Afternoon snack

* Home made fruit yogurt and fruit juice.
* Carrot cake, milk or fruit juice.
* Stewed fruit, homemade custard or yogurt, milk.
* Ice cream and biscuits, fruit juice.
* Home made buns, fruit juice.

Chapter Nine
Safety

The management of a day nursery is responsible for the safety of all children and adults on the nursery premises. This includes children, parents, staff (whether paid or unpaid), observers and visitors.

Accidents usually are, as the word implies, unfortunate chance mishaps. In some cases accidents can be described as unforeseeable or unavoidable in that they are caused by over-exuberance on the part of a child and cannot be directly linked to any failure on the part of staff. For example children may simply fall over their own feet or fall awkwardly off a piece of equipment and sprain or break a limb. Provided precautions have been taken and the children are constantly supervised, then an accident, while it is regrettable, is nonetheless an accident.

Other accidents can be prevented and are a result of negligence. Accidents caused by negligence may be a child falling from a window or pulling a kettle of boiling liquid on top of herself/himself. In such cases, negligence is to blame, and the final responsibility lies with the manager or jointly with the managers of the nursery.

It is vital therefore that:

* all measures be taken to avoid accidents
* procedures be laid down in the case of accidents
* adequate accident insurance be taken out.

Avoiding Accidents

When examining premises or equipment from the point of view of safety, the manager must be very vigilant. If there is even the slightest risk of an accident being caused by an element of the building or its contents, the manager must take every possible precaution to prevent it. All possible sources of danger in the premises, fittings and equipment must be checked, it's no good simply hoping for the best.

The manager and her staff must use common sense and learn to differentiate between high and low risk activities. If a child is hammering a nail with a light hammer s/he is risking a sore finger but learning a lot about hand-eye coordination. If, on the other hand, the child is about to experiment on another child's head then it is time to call a halt. Some activities are not inherently dangerous, but require constant supervision. Many activities such as climbing and learning to ride a bike are not dangerous unless the child is allowed to take unnecessary risks. If, for example, certain children are inclined to climb too high on the climbing frame, they should be encouraged to go no higher than their ability to climb down. Children must have rules and be taught to abide by them, such as 'no climbing on the climbing frame holding a toy.'

Teach the children to think about their own and others' safety. Help them to understand how accidents come about and consider their possible consequences. For example if a child is swinging on two legs of a chair explain what is likely to happen and demonstrate, with an empty chair, what might happen. If the child persists and does fall, resist saying 'I told you so', but comfort the child and then use the opportunity to talk about why it is forbidden to swing on two legs of the chair. Explain to the children that they must not behave in a dangerous manner on the slide, climbing frame etc as they pose a danger to others as well as themselves. Some children do not want to appear to be afraid of injury as they equate fear of injury with cowardice. They can be trained to see the activity as a danger to younger children and so develop their sense of responsibility.

Children should be taught the following basic rules of safety:

* Never run or walk with an object such as a pencil or lollipop stick in your mouth.
* Never play with plastic bags.
* Be careful using scissors.
* Do not touch electricity sockets or plugs.
* Do not slam doors as you can catch your fingers in the doors.
* Teach children how to cross the road in safety.

It may not be possible to anticipate all accidents but it is important to try. Be aware of danger without being too preoccupied with it and take every possible precaution to prevent it. When an accident happens a child, many people experience a sense of guilt especially if the accident was preventable. If you have sincerely done your informed best then you cannot hold yourself totally responsible.

The following is a short list of the types of things to look out for in order to minimise the risks of accident. As every situation and operation is different, this list cannot be exhaustive.

Figure 2: Accident Prevention

Problem	Possible Solution
* Loose or splintered floorboards	* Repair or cover with fitted carpet
* Windows easily opened/opening out	* Window locks or grills fitted inside
* Patio doors and large windows	* Fit safety glass and plastic film to lower section
* Steps and stairs	* Guard with Stair Gate or build shallow ramp on steps
* Climbable railings	* Cover with fine mesh fencing
* Horizontal banisters	* Change to vertical banisters
* Pond	* Remove or cover with strong, fine grid
* Tricycle handle bars unprotected	* Remove until cover is found or replaced
* Wooden swing and see-saw seat	* Replace with rubber seat or cover with old tyre
* Cording set on curtains	* Remove cord, check also that curtains are fire resistant
* Trailing flexes	* Prevent access for children and replace all flexes with curled flexes
* Loose rugs or mats on floor (wood or carpeted)	* Remove or fix to floor
* Double doors between rooms	* Fix one door closed.
* Children climbing on play garage to reach a high shelf	* Fix garage to large sheet of white melamine or to low table
* Stacking toy with stick	* Discard the stick and use the beads as threading toy or glue base and stick to work surface

* Small pegs, beads etc	* Do not use unless you can confine to work area to which babies do not have access
* Very sunny garden	* Have screened area for babies to play in, be sure to have sun block of at least factor 10

Always buy the best possible toys and equipment you can afford. Be sure to repair or remove worn equipment. Cheap toys tend to be less safe than good brand name toys. With expensive toys, you are generally paying for the safety research and general quality of the product. They also tend to last longer and usually come with a guarantee. It is recommended that you buy from a reputable source to be sure you have a contact in case of problems.

Day-to-day Guidelines

* **Do not** let children run about in stocking feet on polished floors.
* **Do not** let children move about holding a glass or any pointed objects such as pencils, or liquids which, if spilled, could cause a slippy wet patch, etc.
* **Do not** use a pillow for babies.
* **Do not** use blankets which have a fringe.
* **Do not** dress babies in loose knit or crochet matinee jackets.
* **Do not** have ribbons or tassels on baby clothes and do not use them for tying soothers to baby clothes. If a baby arrives in the nursery with any such items, remove them and explain the reasons to the parents. It is better to risk embarrassing the parents than to compromise the children's safety.
* **Do not** prop up bottles to let children feed themselves.
* **Do not** carry babies up and down stairs frequently.
* **Do not** leave a baby in a bouncing cradle on a table or work-top.
* **Do not** walk about the room while carrying hot drinks, always sit on the floor at child level.
* **Do not** leave children unsupervised and never leave young children alone with a baby.
* Advise parents not to drive with unrestrained children in the car and remind them never to hold a child in the front seat.

All the staff should have at least a basic knowledge of coping with the following situations:

> Choking or suffocation
> Scalds or burns
> Falls and head injuries
> Poisoning
> Cuts

A **First Aid Box** should be kept out of the reach of the children. Recommended contents include:

> A pair of sharp scissors.
> A pair of tweezers.
> Cotton wool.
> Safety pins.
> Antiseptic cream.
> Adhesive plasters.
> First Aid tape.
> Butterfly closures.
> Sterilised swabs.
> Eye and finger bandages.
> I", 2" and 3" wide bandages.
> 2" crepe bandages.
> Cleanser for washing wounds.
> Burn dressing (not for serious burns).
> Eye-bath.
> Temperature strips.
> Small bar of antiseptic soap.
> Analgesic (for stings).
> A cotton pad soaked in water can be kept in the freezer for use as an ice-pack.

No prescribed medicines should be administered to children without their parents' written permission. Paracetomol elixir such as Calpol should be available in case of emergency. All medicines should be administered on a measured spoon supplied for the purpose. Medicines must be kept out of children's reach. If they are stored in a low fridge they should be fitted with child-proof caps. It should be arranged that a local General Practitioner will be 'on call' to attend at the nursery in case of emergency. A good reference guide to children's illnesses and symptoms should be close at hand. *See Recommended Reading.*

Fire Prevention

The Fire Prevention Officer will be able to give more detailed advice in individual cases. The following are some general guidelines designed to cover a wide range of organisational and management procedures to avoid the occurrence of fire and to ensure that correct action will be taken by management and staff in the event of an outbreak of fire.

General

1 Maintain escape routes so that they can be safely and effectively used at all times.
2 Staircases must be totally enclosed with $^1/_2$ hour fire resistant door fitted with self closing device with direct access to the open air.
3 Smoke alarms should be fitted.
4 Staff should be trained in fire drill.
5 Designate staff responsible for fire safety.
6 There should be adequate staff to facilitate evacuation.
7 Keep records of who is in the building.
8 Wall covering should be of non-combustible material. There should be no timber or cork lining.
9 Good housekeeping can help prevent occurrences likely to constitute a fire hazard, for instance ensure safe disposal of waste, safe storage of flammables such as oil, polish etc.
10 All soft toys, furnishings and curtains should be of fire resistant materials.
11 Clean the chimney twice a year.

Electricity

1 Electricity wiring should be new and must meet all safety standards.
2 Do not use multiway adapters.
3 Regularly check flexes and replace any which are frayed.
4 Reduce the risk of fire by having a circuit breaker safety device installed (ELCB).

Gas

1 Switch off supply if you suspect a leak, and contact the gas company.
2 Check flexible hoses and couplings on cylinders for signs of

wear and replace if they are worn.
3   Ensure that rooms with a gas heater have adequate ventilation.
4   Store cylinders upright and outside.

If an Accident Happens

Unfortunately accidents do happen and it is advisable to have a definite procedure for such an eventuality.

*   Emergency telephone numbers should be posted by the phone. These should include the Emergency Services, nursery doctor, transport, and stand-by helpers.
*   The children's details, including home or contact phone numbers, should be close to hand. In the case of a serious accident, these details should be sent with the child in the Ambulance.
*   There should be a well stocked First Aid Box. (*See Above*)
*   At all times, there must a be at least one member of the staff on duty who has a knowledge of basic First Aid.

Hints on First Aid

This advice is concerned only with First Aid which is the treating of a casualty in the period before s/he is placed in the care of trained medical help. If medical help is going to be needed it is imperative that it be called at once.

What to do in an emergency

1   Do not panic.
2   Send staff to phone emergency services and/or doctor and/or parents.
3   Check the child's record card for allergies (*See Figure 11: Sample record card* on page 107).
4   In a life threatening situation, remember the ABC of life support:
Airways open: open and maintain the victim's breathing.
Breathing restored: if the victim is not breathing, begin resuscitation at once.
Circulation maintained: if there is no pulse, begin cardiac massage.
5   Check for bleeding - Apply pressure or treat wound.

6 Look for signs of shock and fractures. Do not move victim.
7 Keep the victim quiet and warm.
8 Do not give an unconscious person anything to drink.

Dressing a surface wound

1 Wash your hands thoroughly.
2 Cleanse the wound and surrounding area gently with mild antiseptic soap and water. Rinse with clean running water if possible, pat dry with sterile pad.
3 Treat to prevent contamination.
4 Cover with sterile lint dressing or pad. Secure with tape.
5 If the victim has not had tetanus immunization it should be recommended (to the parents).

DEEP WOUNDS AND SERIOUS BURNS SHOULD BE TREATED ONLY BY PROFESSIONAL MEDICAL PERSONNEL. WHILE WAITING FOR THE ARRIVAL OF A DOCTOR OR AMBULANCE, TREAT FOR BLEEDING AND SHOCK.

Bleeding

1 Control bleeding with pressure pad of sterilised lint dressing or clean cloth.
2 Lie patient down and raise the injured area higher than the patient's heart. Keep the patient warm.
3 Maintain an open airway. If victim vomits, gently turn head to side.
4 Get medical help immediately.

Burns and Scalds

NB Do not clean burns or break blisters.
Do not remove any clothing which has adhered to the burn.
Do not apply grease, ointment or medication to a serious burn.
Do not use cotton wool or anything with loose fibres to cover burns.

First degree burns: Redness or discolouration of skin surface, mild swelling and pain.
1 Cool area with cool running water, immerse area or pat area with cool, wet cloths. Do not use ice.
2 Blot gently. Apply a light, dry dressing if necessary.

Second degree burns: Deep burns with red or mottled appearance; blisters; considerable pain and swelling. Skin surface appears wet. Treat as for first degree burns.

Third degree burns: Deep tissue destruction with a white or charred appearance; no pain.
1 Treat for shock.
2 Do not touch or lean or breathe over the burned area.
3 Arrange transportation to hospital *immediately*.

Eyes

Foreign bodies in the eyes should be removed with great care using a piece of cotton soaked in cold water.

If the object is not easily removed cover lightly with a sterile lint dressing and seek medical attention.

Broken Bone (Fracture)

1 If a broken bone is suspected **do not** move victim until a splint has been applied, except in a life threatening situation.
2 Seek medical attention immediately.
3 Treat for shock.

Stings

1 If the sting has been left in skin, remove it using tweezers or by gently scraping with fingernail. Do not squeeze.
2 Apply antiseptic cream.
3 For multiple stings, soak affected area in a cool bath to which has been added 1 teaspoonful of baking soda per quart of water.
4 If severe allergic reactions appear get medical assistance.

Sunburn

1 Treat as for minor burns (see above).
2 Treat for shock if necessary.
3 Cool victim as soon as possible in cool (not cold) bath.
4 Give plenty of fluids to drink if not in shock.
5 Get medical attention.

Shock

NB Shock is a dangerous condition and can be fatal. Expect some degree of shock in any emergency.

Symptoms may include: unusual weakness or fainting; cold, pale, clammy skin; rapid weak pulse; shallow irregular breathing; chills; nausea or unconsciousness.

Treatment:

1 Treat known cause of shock as quickly as possible, ie breathing difficulty, bleeding.
2 Maintain an open airway. If victim vomits gently turn head to the side.
3 Keep patient warm and lying flat.
4 Get medical help immediately.
5 **Do not** give anything by mouth.

Head injury

1 If a child sustains a blow to the head treat any minor cuts as above.
2 If the child is playing normally within 10-15 seconds there should be no need to worry but supervise the child for other symptoms.
3 If the child complains of a mild headache but is otherwise alert, let her or him lie down in a darkened room for about one hour. Supervise the child for other symptoms.
4 A head injury which results in any of the following should be treated as an emergency:
   severe headache
   causes the child to be dazed, stunned or drowsy
   loss of consciousness
   irritability
   vomiting
   discharge of blood or straw-coloured fluid from the nose or ears
   The child may have suffered concussion or a fractured skull.
   Seek medical assistance.

Accident Records

Accident Records should be kept and the details of every accident, however slight, must be recorded. The accident records will highlight for management and staff any 'accident black spots' in the nursery. Every effort must be made to prevent accidents recurring. Staff supervising children must be able to tell in detail exactly how an accident occurred. It is not acceptable for a parent to be told "Johnny has a black eye, don't know how it happened but he seems OK!"

Figure 3: Accident Record Card

Date _____   Time _____

Room or area in which accident occurred

_____

Name of child/children involved in accident

_____

Nature of injury

_____

Action taken

_____

By whom _____

Was medical attention required? _____

Who was called _____

By whom _____

Who witnessed accident

_____

Who informed parents

_____

Who was on duty

_____

Signed

_____

Any other comments:

_____

_____

Fire Routine for Staff

All staff should be involved in fire drill on a regular basis and a member of staff appointed fire officer with responsibility for fire prevention and fire drill organisation.

Fire Routine as a general rule should be based on the following sequence of events:

1 Raise alarm
2 Call Fire Brigade.
3 Evacuation.
4 Assembly.
5 Staff report to Fire Officer.
6 Attack fire.

While details will vary depending on the circumstances of each nursery, the following list will assist you in developing a fire routine.

* RAISE ALARM
    Choose the type of fire alarm most suitable to the nursery premises. For example, choose between audible sirens or flashing lights and single or two-stage alarms, and decide how much of the building needs to be connected to the alarm system.
* CALL FIRE BRIGADE
    Give precise address and directions, including name of nearest main road and/or other landmarks.
* EVACUATION
    Set regulations about closing doors and windows; isolating power and/or gas, ie turn off electricity and gas where possible; thorough check of toilets, sleeping room etc.
* ASSEMBLY
    Designate an assembly point away from building. Carry out a roll call.
* STAFF REPORTING
    All staff should report to the designated nursery fire officer. The nursery fire officer updates Fire Brigade upon arrival.
* ATTACKING FIRE
    Should only be done by trained personnel and only without personal risk.

Insurance

It is imperative that every day nursery take out a comprehensive insurance policy. This safeguards the nursery from any claims which may arise in the event of an accident. The insurance cover you choose must be adequate and take into account the fact that you are insuring mainly children who will have a high life expectancy.

The usual types of insurance are:

* Property insurance.
* Public liability.
* Employer liability.
* Personal accident.
* Loss of money.

Property insurance, public liability and employer liability must be arranged and in operation before you open your premises to be used or visited by prospective staff or parents. Insurance can be arranged through an Insurance Broker and it is important that you provide the broker with accurate information about your nursery. Check the maximum child/staff ratio, if you go above this ratio you will no longer be insured. If one member of your staff is absent at any time, will you still be insured? What if two members of staff are absent? Are you insured for outings? If one of the nursery carers brings a child to the shops, is this covered? What are you not covered for? Do not presume you are covered, if in doubt ask your broker. Read your policy very carefully ... especially the exclusion clauses.

Health insurance, insurance against personal accident and insurance against loss (of money or contents of freezers etc) may not be obligatory but in some cases they may be desirable. Again check with your broker who will be able to advise - but will no doubt be eager to sell you as much insurance as possible.

If you have dependants or if you are the main or sole earner in your family you will need to consider providing for two possibilities:

a   Funds for yourself and your family after your retirement.
    and
b   Funds for your dependants upon your death.

Personal Pension Plans (PPPs) are necessary if a self-employed person wants to maintain a certain standard of living after retirement. A pension plan is not a luxury item, for many self-employed it may be the only thing which enables them to afford to retire.

As well as being a long-term investment which will provide you with an income after you retire, a pension plan also offers attractive tax relief in the shorter term. All the money paid into PPPs is tax-free and the funds accrued are also tax free. Apart from the tax relief and investment potential of PPPs they also provide tax-free lump sum options at retirement and also death benefits in the event of death before retirement. This may be essential if the nursery manager has dependants.

Naturally there is a limit to the amount a person can pay into PPPs and at the moment the limit is approximately 15% of taxable earnings. The pension fund itself also remains free from both income and capital gains taxes.

Life Assurance provides funds for your dependents upon your death. As with PPPs moneys paid to life assurance are eligible for tax relief.

Before choosing any type of assurance or pension plan it is recommended that you contact a personal financial broker who will be able to give you advice based on your own requirements.

Chapter Ten
Hygiene

Hygiene is of the utmost importance in a day nursery. While it is to be expected that some childhood illnesses are inevitably going to affect the children in the nursery at one time or another, many illnesses can, and should, be prevented. The first line of defence will be taken by the parents. The parents should endeavour to have their child immunised against as many illnesses as possible. Many nurseries insist on a minimum immunisation, unless there are contra indications in individual children, for example MMR (Measles, Mumps, Rubella); 3-in-1 (Diphtheria, Tetanus, Whooping cough); BCG (Tuberculosis); Polio.

The second line of defence against infections will be taken by the nursery. This should be done in two main ways:

1 By maintaining high hygiene standards.
2 By conscientious insistence that any child who has been absent through illness will only be readmitted with a doctor's certificate confirming that the child is no longer infectious or contagious.

A good cleaning and sterilising routine in the nursery will reduce the risk of gastric and other illnesses. It is not enough that the nursery premises be clean, the staff must also be aware and be meticulous about their personal hygiene. The premises should be easily maintained at a high level of hygiene.

* *Food* must be prepared, stored and handled properly. All foods should be freshly and hygienically prepared on a daily basis. Food should not be saved and reheated for serving another day. Many parents like to be responsible for their child's food, especially in the early years. In this case the parents may supply puree food for their baby. This must be labelled and kept in the fridge for use that day. Parents may continue to supply infant food until the child is able to eat the same diet as the other children. If a freezer is available the parents may bring a week's supply of frozen baby-food at the beginning of each week. This food should be transported in an insulated bag to avoid thawing and refreezing. It is desirable that baby bottles be prepared in the children's homes, but if they are to be prepared in the nursery careful hand-washing by staff must be adhered to and a

high standard of hygiene enforced.
* Ideally food should not be prepared by the member of staff assigned to nappy changing duties. Food Hygiene Regulations require that no sanitary convenience communicates directly with a room or other place which is used for food preparation or eating. This means that there must be a room or corridor between the dining room and toilet/nappy changing area. Be sure there are adequate cooking facilities.

It is up to the management of each nursery to lay down rules of hygiene. Some nurseries will have staff exclusively looking after cleaning and cooking, while in smaller nurseries the child-minding staff may have to share these tasks. In these cases the staff will have to be especially aware of hygiene. All staff must be careful that children do not share cups or spoons at tables and that babies do not share bottles, soothers or bibs.

Nursery staff should have access to books on hygiene and these should be required reading in every nursery. *See Recommended Reading* for further guidelines.

Chapter Eleven
Budgeting

Before your nursery begins to trade you must anticipate, as far as possible, how it will operate financially. This is known as budgeting. When the nursery is up and running you must continue to budget month to month and annually.

Good budgeting and record keeping is designed to prevent the following:

* Overextending. Taking on too many children could result in increased overheads.
* Incorrect calculation of prices.
* Business slipping into a loss-making situation and not being realised for some time.
* Places being held but not being paid for.

Figure 4 shows a list of expenses which should be considered when budgeting. These expenses will ultimately determine the fees which must be generated by the nursery in order that to keep the business viable. The *total* is the break-even point, ie it is the minimum amount which must be received so that the nursery does not accumulate debt. Any amount above this figure is profit.

When calculating the fees to be charged by your nursery, you should only consider your own expenses. There is no benefit to be derived from matching your fees to those of other nurseries. The charges at other nurseries may be lower than yours because they do not have the same overheads. For example, they may have a lower mortgage or rent, or different standards of food or staff and are thus in a position to charge lower fees. If you try to match their fees in order to be 'competitive' you may very soon be out of business and deep in debt. Bear in mind that your overheads may be higher because your standards are higher, so if you feel inclined to compare your fees to other nurseries try to establish if you are comparing like with like. However, if you feel that the fees which you have calculated are prohibitive, you must reduce your expenses to bring your fees to an affordable level for your clients.

Figure 4: Expenses

Rent/Mortgage

Rates

Wages

Catering and toiletries

Teaching aids and equipment

Light and heat

Phone

Post and stationery

Advertising

Car expenses

Repair and maintenance of building

Security

Insurance

Accounting

Bank charges and interest

TOTAL

Your cash flow should enable you to see immediately if *monies received* are balanced by *payments made*:

Figure 5: Cash Flow

MONTH	Jan	Feb	...	Nov	Dec
RECEIPTS					
Fees Received					
Loans Received					
Other Received					
A Total Received					
PAYMENTS					
Rent					
Mortgage					
Rates					
Wages					
Catering					
Teaching aids					
Light/Heat					
Phone					
Post/Stationery					
Advertising					
Motor					
Repair/Maintenance					
Insurances					
Audit/Accountancy					
Bank Charges					
Sundry Expenses					
B Total Payments					
A-B = Surplus					

It is not mandatory to begin trading in any particular month. Many nurseries begin to take children in September as this is the beginning of the school year, but another month such as January or February may suit you better. It is not advisable to open a nursery in December, June, July or August as these are holiday times. You may have difficulty filling places during holiday times, and you could also be faced with the problem of settling the same children into the nursery twice over a short space of time, first when they start in the nursery and again when they return after the holidays.

It is important not to be too optimistic about attendance when budgeting and it is better to err on the side of caution. When calculating fees you should allow for absenteeism. Unfortunately it is difficult to predict exactly what illness you may have in the nursery from week to week let alone a year in advance. As a general guideline, you could initially allow for four weeks holidays in the year per child and, for larger groups, at least one child absent per day. In later years you will have more information available to you from your own records, and this will enable you to budget more accurately.

Do not feel too rushed to open. Make sure that you are well prepared and don't open until you are ready, even if it means waiting until next year. It is most important that you have had a lot of practical experience before you do eventually open a day nursery. You would not consider yourself a gourmet chef after reading a cookery book no more than you can consider yourself qualified to open and run a day nursery without a number of years' experience.

Financing Your Venture

Before you approach a financial institution for funding you must prepare a Business Plan. This plan is your proposal to the financial institution explaining why you feel you have a viable business idea. It is designed to convey in writing your qualities as a business woman and your level of professional and business acumen. It must therefore be clearly presented and contain as much information as possible. It should contain the following:

Description of your proposed nursery

Give a detailed description of the type of service you intend to offer. This should include hours of opening, numbers and ages of children, qualifications and number of staff, details of fees etc. If you have a brochure prepared, it should be enclosed. A business forecast should also be included.

Information about proposed nursery manager

Give details of the manager's areas of expertise and qualifications. Outline how these areas of expertise will be used in the management structure. Describe whether the nursery will have a single manager or be run as a partnership, co-operative or voluntary committee. Provide details of your existing banking history, if any.

Target market

Details of your prospective clientele. Are you situated near their homes or work? Are there any other nurseries in the area and are they turning away children or do they constitute competition? Provide results of any market research you have carried out.

Clients

Outline the number of children you will take on initially and projected figures for future years. Describe how you intend to attract clients, what advertising you are going to use, if any.

Fees

State fees to be charged and how these fees relate to the incomes of your potential clients.

The Bank

Your local bank manager may be a source of advice as well as finance. S/he will furnish you with publications which will guide you in book keeping in a small business. The Industrial Development Authority (Ireland) or similar body can help with advice and support.

The two types of finance normally available to a small business are the **Overdraft** and the **Term Loan**.

Overdraft

An overdraft is normally the cheapest and most flexible form of borrowing. Interest is charged daily and only while the facility is being used. There is not usually any requirement to repay the overdraft in a fixed period but this can be a disadvantage as interest is not easily predetermined. Most banks review a client's overdraft facilities annually at least. Surcharges can apply if the account is not in credit for one month in twelve.

Term Loan

The term loan is slightly more expensive than an overdraft but the loan is for a fixed amount over a fixed period. For this reason it may be preferable to an overdraft as it enables you to budget for predetermined costs. Loans are usually for fixed periods of three, five or seven years and repayments are usually made monthly, quarterly or half-yearly.

The term loan should be taken out as near to the start-up date as possible as you will be required to begin repayments at the end of the first month, quarter or half year.

Financial Planning

Every businesswoman must be concerned with three main areas of financial planning:

* Setting up a basic record system to monitor earnings and expenditure. *See Figure 5: Cash Flow.*
* Budgeting to assess the financial performance of the business and to anticipate any problems which may arise.
* Setting up a benefits package to include insurances and pension to protect herself, her business and employees. *See Chapter Nine.*

Keeping Records

A record-keeping system is most important. It lets you monitor closely how you are performing financially. A good record-keeping system should show:

* How much money you have received.
* How much money you have spent.
* How much you are owed and by whom.
* How much you owe and to whom.

You will also need orderly and clear records if you wish to obtain financial support from financial institutions or social services. (*See Chapter Eleven*).

Likewise, you will need clear records for tax purposes. It is important that you are able to differentiate between income and turnover. For tax purposes you may have to justify all pre-tax deductions and demonstrate them as valid business expenses to your accountant or the tax inspector.

Records are the basic evidence of all business transactions. Every document relating to financial transactions must be retained - this includes invoices, bank statements, cheque stubs and till receipts. It is strongly recommended that you establish some system for filing these, either in order of date, reference numbers or alphabetically. Whatever system you use must be easy to use, up-to-date and accurate.

Choose a system appropriate to your needs for record keeping. A single book may be sufficient, or you may choose to use a computer. Always keep your records up to date and in a safe place. Whether your records are managed by yourself or by someone else, such as a secretary, partner or accountant, you must remain familiar with whatever system is used because it is important that you can extract and understand the information which has been collated. Lack of financial control is one of the most common weaknesses in the management of small businesses.

Your Business in Brief

The minimum information you will need to know about your business is:

*   How much money is due to come in - **debtors.**
*   How much you are due to pay out - **creditors.**

The aim of a viable business is to ensure that the amount due from you debtors is greater than the amount you owe your creditors.

In the nursery your debtors' book is the roll book. This serves as both a record of attendance and fees received. Because the nursery is not generally involved in large turnover in stock the cheque analysis book can serve as your creditors' book. Payments should be confined to cheque payments but if cash is generally used, a cash analysis book will be required.

Invoices must be retained and filed with a note of the serial number of the cheque used for payment. If cash is used the reference number from the cash analysis book should be noted.

A wages book should also be kept, containing details of PAYE, National Insurance and PRSI. Employer registration forms are available from your local tax office and they will also supply a copy of the *Employer's Guide To PAYE and PRSI* (Ireland) or the *Inland Revenue New Employers Starters Pack* (Britain). These publications are very helpful and easy to follow. They contain some information on other benefits to which your employees may at some time become entitled.

VAT accounts may be required if the turnover of the non-school element of the nursery (being a service) is likely to exceed a set amount in a year. The school or pre-school element of the nursery may be exempt from VAT. The revenue commissioners will supply a *Guide To The Value Added Tax* containing up-to-date information on this subject.

If you are trading under a name other than your own, you are required to register the name with your local registrar of business names. You may also be obliged to display this name on your premises.

If you are contemplating forming a limited company you will require expert advice from a solicitor or accountant or a company specialising in the formation of companies. The cost for this advice can range from about £200 for a company 'off the peg' to about £400 for a made to-measure-company. It is recommended that you take expert advice before forming a limited company as there are both advantages and disadvantages to operating as a limited company.

Finance and Costing

An exercise in diminishing returns is important for demonstrating that bigger is not always better, financially speaking.

You will find that while profits may be enhanced significantly by increasing the number of children from, for example, five to ten, further increases in numbers of children may not enhance profits proportionally and may even result in the nursery running at a loss.

As the number of children increases so do some of the variable expenses. Having more children in the nursery means having to hire more staff, using more food and increasing wear and tear in the nursery. Completing this chart will show the minimum number of children required to pay overheads which do not vary significantly or not at all, ie mortgage or rent, rates etc.

Figure 6: Diminishing returns

Fees received per week	Anticipated number of children attending							
	5	10	15	20	25	30	35	..
£25	125	250	375	500	625	750	875	..
£30	150	300	450	600	750	900	1050	..
£35	175	350	525	700	875	1050	1225	..
£40	200	400	600	800	1000	1200	1400	..
£45	225	450	675	900	1125	1350	1575	..
£50	250	500	750	1000	1250	1500	1750	..
Fixed Expenses								
Rates								
Rent/Mortgage								
Insurances								
Audit/ Accountancy								
Security								
TOTAL								
Variable Expenses								
Wages								
Catering								
Teaching aids								
Light/Heat								
Phone								
Post/Stationery								
Advertising								
Car Expenses								
Repair/ Maintenance								
Bank Charges								
Sundry Expenses								
TOTAL								

Weekly Roll Book

The nursery manager may not be in a position to spend time away from the children managing day to day accounts. It is vital that the roll book contain as much information as possible and that this information is clearly and simply presented. Figure 7 shows a roll book for a two week period, before and after fees have been taken in.

Figure 7: Roll Book

Monday Morning

Child's name	1 Previous fees due	2 This wk's fees	3 Other dues	4 Total	5 Cheque payments	6 Cash payments	7 Balance due
Mary	£30	£30	—				
John	—	£30	—				
Simon	—	£30	—				
Sara	—	£30	£5				
David	£30	£30	£5				

Thursday Morning

Child's name	1 Previous fees due	2 This wk's fees	3 Other dues	4 Total	5 Cheque payments	6 Cash payments	7 Balance due
John	—	£30	—	£30	£30	—	—
Mary	£30	£30	—	£60	—	£60	—
Simon	—	£30	£5	£30	£30	—	£30
Sara	—	£30	£5	£35	£30	—	£5
David	£30	£30	£5	£65	£35	—	£30

The system: As each parent pays fees and any other money due, the amount is entered into columns 5 or 6. There should be no need for the manager to spend any time with the books at this stage. She should do no more than enter the amount received and put the money safely aside.

Before a lodgment is made on, for example every Friday afternoon, the columns are added thus:

Columns
John $(1 + 2 + 3) = 4 = (5 + 6 + 7)$
Mary $(1 + 2 + 3) = 4 = (5 + 6 + 7)$ *etc*

If $1 + 2 + 3$ does not equal $5 + 6 + 7$ then you have possibly:

> omitted to enter fees not yet received into column 7
> *or*
> received more than anticipated, perhaps a week's fees in advance for next week.

If the second option is the case, ie you have received a week's fees in advance, then this amount should be entered in column 3 and next week column 2 will be 'nil' for that child. This week's column 7 is the same as next week's column 1.

This system will quickly show any discrepancies.

It is not advisable to allow unpaid fees to accumulate. If parents have trouble paying this week's fees it will be more difficult for them to pay double fees next week. If parents are themselves paid monthly they may prefer to pay their fees monthly (four or five weekly) in advance. In such cases you will have fees in columns 2 and 5 this week but 'nil' or 'paid' in these columns for the next four or five weeks.

The nursery should be wary of offering reductions to some parents and not to others. Parents paying full fees can feel that they are subsidising places which are given at reduced cost and this can lead to resentment. While some parents will not mind reductions being offered in exceptional cases of need they do not like to feel that a proportion of the parents are subsidising a significant number of places. Depending on circumstances, certain parents may be entitled to some assistance with nursery fees through Social Welfare.

The nursery itself may become non-viable if there are too many reductions. If a number of places in the nursery are reserved to be offered at reduced cost other parents should be aware of this and these reductions accounted for in the budgeting.

Figure 8: Cheque Analysis Book

Cheque to	Cheque Number	Total	PAYE/ Wages	Catering	Heat & Light	Car	Drawings
M Black	1	£100	£100				
A Brown	2	£120	£120				
Collector General	3	£70	£70				
Quinnsworth	4	£50		£50			
Conoco Oil	5	£250			£250		
P Marks	6	£25					£25
Esso	7	£10				£10	
To cash	8	£15		£9		£3	£3
Sox finance co	9	£25				£25	

Column 1 records the name of the person to whom the cheque is paid or the type of bank withdrawal, eg Standing order, direct debit, bank charges.

Column 2: records the serial number on the cheque stub. This number will be noted on receipts and invoices and checked against your Bank Statement (*See Bank Reconciliation*).

Column 3: is the total amount for which the cheque is written.

Column 4 to end: are the breakdown of how the payment relates to the business.

In this example:

Cheque number 1: Has been paid in total to 'M Black', an employee, so is recorded as a business expense.
Cheques 2,3,4, and *5* were also business expenses.
Cheque number 6: was paid to P Marks for a hair-cut and is not normally considered a legitimate business expense and is therefore treated as a drawing.*
Cheque number 7: was for petrol (as can be seen from the receipt from the petrol station filed under 'Petrol' or 'Car'). This is usually allowable as a business expense in the proportion in which the car is used for business and private purposes and is apportioned at the end of the financial year.
Cheque number 8: was cash drawn from the bank and was used partly for business, (£12) and partly for drawings (£3).*
Cheque number 9: this is a car loan repayment usually allowable as a business expense as for cheque number 7.

> * *Note*: In this example the manager has taken £28 as drawings, ie she has paid herself £28. She must be careful that the business has earned £28 or is guaranteed to earn this amount over and above the amount she is still due to pay (which she can assess from her Invoices Book or the pile of bills on her table, depending on the system she uses.) Be careful of cash-in-hand, it is not your money until all bills have been paid. In order to avoid confusing personal expenditure with business expenditure it is sensible for the manager to run two separate bank accounts.

It is important that you keep your cheque analysis book up-to-date, any cheques written and any withdrawals must be entered in this book before you can do a bank reconciliation.

When you receive your bank statement the balance on the statement may not be the same as your records. The difference may be accounted for by lodgments, withdrawals or cheques written which have not been put through your account by the bank at the time your statement was being issued. To confirm the actual situation on your account, you must carry out a bank reconciliation.

To do this you will need your:

> Cheque analysis book.
> Cheque book.
> Lodgments book.
> Records of withdrawals made using an automatic cash dispenser, direct debits, standing orders, etc.

Go through your analysis book and tick off each withdrawal which has been entered on your statement. Any cheque or withdrawal which you have made but does not appear on the statement must be noted.

Go through your lodgments book and tick off each lodgment which has been entered on your statement. Any lodgment made but not appearing on the statement must be noted.

Proceed with the following sum:

Final balance from Statement   _____

+   Any lodgment made but not
appearing on the statement   _____
= Sub-
Total

−   Any cheque or withdrawal made
but not appearing on the statement   _____
= Balance

You may also reconcile your cheque book in the same way. The balance after reconciling the cheque book should be the same as the total in your cheque book. If there are any discrepancies review your own calculations and then re-check the statements. Any differences should be highlighted by this check, and if necessary you should contact your bank.

Chapter Twelve
Marketing and Promotion

Advertising

The two main aims of advertising are:

*   To give information about the service you offer, and
*   To project your nursery's image.

It is not necessary to give a long description of exactly what a day nursery is. It probably goes without saying that a day nursery caters for young children, remains open five days a week and has qualified staff. Compare these advertisements:

Day nursery available, catering for children age one to five years. Open 8am - 6pm, five days per week. Qualified staff. Phone 1234567 for further information.

Day nursery with Montessori pre-school. After-school facilities, including collection. Resident nutritionist, vegetarian food a speciality. For further information phone Sandy at 1234567

With approximately the same number of words the second advertisement gives parents a good idea of what exactly makes this particular nursery different from others. If the family is vegetarian or just interested in healthy eating and / or has school-going children the parents will be more attracted by the second advertisement and will no doubt be eager to visit.

If you advertise in more than one medium (eg national or local newspapers, local shops etc) it is important to compare results from each type of advertising to establish which method is the most successful and more importantly which advertisement is not stimulating interest. This can be done by asking enquirers where they saw your advertisement. Word of mouth is often the best form of advertising and you may find in later years that many enquiries are the result of personal recommendation from parents using your nursery.

In general, advertising can be expensive and the results may be difficult to gauge. When you advertise in the local or national newspapers you may receive enquiries immediately or some time in the future. Immediate enquiries are likely to be from people who are currently looking for a child care service.

Any advertisement can elicit unwanted responses which are only of nuisance value. Though these may be expected, do not let them bother you too much. Nuisance responses may range from obscene calls to fake enquiries. An obscene call should not be responded to at all, just hang up on the caller, and take the phone off the hook if the caller persists. If obscene calls continue you should contact the police.

The fake enquiries are usually from people who ring just to know your business or to compare your prices for the sake of curiosity. These can be difficult to distinguish from genuine enquiries so avoid being rude or abrupt with callers. If you feel that a caller is not a genuine prospective client you should remain polite but try not to let such callers occupy too much of your time.

Day nursery advertising may be done in the following ways:

The National Newspapers.
The Local Newspapers.
Free Newspapers.
Monthly Publications.
Telephone Directory or Yellow Pages.
Shops and Supermarkets.
Direct Mailing or Fliers.

Newspapers

The main advantage of newspaper advertising is that it can reach a large number of people, and local papers can be an effective way of reaching the target market. The target market area is the area from which you expect to get your clientele. It may be the area immediately surrounding the nursery, the nearest suburban area or the nearest place of employment. Some newspapers are identified as being more popular in particular areas, for example, local papers may be preferred to the national papers by prospective clients, and you should bear this in mind when advertising in newspapers. Advertising in national newspapers is more expensive than advertising in local ones.

Newspapers normally have classified, display or personal advertisements. Some papers do not have a specific day nursery category but they may have a column normally used by the child-minding services eg children's nurses, au-pairs or domestics. Before advertising you should become familiar with all the choices. In this way you will be able to judge, for example, which paper is the most popular for day nursery advertisements or if any one day in the week is more popular for day nursery advertising. If you feel that the paper of your choice is confusing in its presentation of the day nursery advertisements, you should write and ask them to give 'Day Nurseries and Child-minding' a section of its own, as distinct from the more general 'Domestics' which has been commonly used.

Advertising in the classified section is less expensive than a display advertisement. The classified advertisement is charged by the number of lines: normally a line contains four or five words. Display advertisements are charged by the number of column centimetres used, ie the charge is based on the width of the advertisement measured in columns multiplied by the length in centimetres, regardless of wording. Personal advertisements are grouped on the inside or back page and are charged by the line. Many papers offer special deals such as four days' advertising for the price of three, and will not charge for cancelled advertisements if given enough notice.

Newspaper advertisements are not durable in that they generally last only as long as the newspaper, ie one day. However people do not always dispose of papers promptly, so the ad is more durable than radio. Also, if people are interested they may cut out and keep the ad.

Free Newspapers

Newspapers which are delivered free to readers' households rely on advertisements as their only source of income, so their advertising rates can be quite high. Free papers generally specialise in display advertising so their classified sections tend not to be as widely read as classifieds in other papers. However, occasionally these papers run special interest articles. If a local paper is running a feature on child care, for instance, your advertisement may reach a large number of people within the target market.

These advertisements are not durable and because the readers may receive the paper at different times in the week/month enquiries may be spread over a period of time. It may be weeks rather than days before you can establish the success or failure of your advertisement.

Although these papers are free to the readers, it is difficult to estimate the actual readership. Despite their large distribution, bear in mind that many people may simply throw the paper away unopened.

Monthly Publications

It is usually very expensive to advertise in the glossier publications. A black and white display advert taking up an eighth of a page in a magazine will cost a couple of hundred pounds, even if you supply the artwork! The target market of most magazines is usually quite specific, it would obviously be of limited value to advertise in something like *Cycling Weekly*. If you take a large advertisement in a magazine, a journalist may be assigned to do an article on your nursery to run in conjunction with your advertisement. Again, magazines may run special interest articles on subjects related to child care, and on these occasions may have a larger readership within your target market. Magazine advertisements are more durable than newspapers as the magazines tend to be kept about the house or office for at least a month. To increase their longevity you might consider purchasing a few copies and donating them to your local doctor, dentist, clinic, and so on.

Telephone directory and yellow pages

In the Yellow Pages there are a number of classifications under which your service could appear eg Schools, Montessori Schools and Kindergartens, Playgroups, Child-minders, etc. You may opt to have your free entry in one section, a simple entry in others and a display advertisement in the most popular section.

An advertisement in the Yellow Pages is good value for money considering that the advertisement is as durable as the book. A half-inch display advertisement is more expensive than a simple entry. Artwork, your logo for example, will add to the expense. If you are the only nursery in your area you may feel there is little point in spending large sums on an expensive advertisement.

You may, on the other hand, like to portray the professionalism of your nursery by having a professional display advertisement with text and logo. Most printing companies can advise on printing headed notepaper and business cards. The artwork on your notepaper and cards can normally be used in any display advertisement.

Shops and supermarkets

It may be useful to put a notice in local shops and supermarkets as there is usually no charge. Though they may not be durable they can be renewed. It is a good idea to have cards printed specially for this purpose. These cards can be slightly larger than normal business cards and should specify where you are located and precisely what the nursery offers, some artwork may also be worthwhile to attract people to read your card. It is not normally feasible or necessary to pack too much information on the card.

Making a Good Impression

Your first contact with clients is likely to be a *phone conversation*, and on the basis of this conversation your clients will form their first impression of the nursery. So a good telephone manner is important to make a good impression.

If the phone is in a room where there is activity and noise, do not answer it. Happy noise can sound like pure chaos over the phone! It is sensible to have an extension phone in the hall or office rather than in the play or dining rooms.

If the phone rings when you are busy, leave it. It can give a very bad impression if you sound harassed and out-of-breath when you answer the phone. The nursery will initially be judged by this first encounter. If you sound confident and assured on the phone then callers are likely to assume that you are confident and competent with children.

Particular members of staff should be assigned to answer the phone in your absence. This alleviates the problem of junior staff giving misinformation due to their inexperience and shyness. If a junior member of staff is unlikely to be of assistance to clients, answering the phone will only distract her from her charges.

Whoever answers the phone should be authorised to handle all enquiries. She should be familiar with the booking list, vacancies etc. If a call is related to the business side of the nursery or some aspect of the nursery with which the person answering the phone is not familiar, she should not attempt to discuss these matters. She should tell the caller that you are not available and take a message.

Nursery personnel must not give out confidential information such as the home addresses or phone numbers of other members of staff, or of children or their parents. If, for example, the mother of one of the children wants to contact the mother of one of the other children, you should offer to pass on the message for her instead of giving her the phone number.

If you are unable to come to the phone, it is preferable for callers to be told that you are 'unavailable' rather than 'out'. The term 'unavailable' suggests that you are busy while to be 'out' implies you are have left your duties and gone off for the day! You may limit the times you are available to specific hours so that you have uninterrupted times with the children. For example a caller can be told that you are involved in an activity with the children and will be unavailable until 3 o'clock.

The phone should not intrude on the children's activities more than is strictly necessary. If there are not enough staff available to tend to the phone it may be worth investing in an answering machine or in some way limiting phone enquiries to specific times. It could be stated on advertisements that phone calls should be between specified times or in the evening. But remember that this type of instruction might make parents think that the staff are so overworked there is no one to answer the phone, which may unfortunately be the truth.

Prepare in advance what you will say to enquirers and try to limit the time you spend on the phone and away from the children. Unless you have the extra staff or are not very busy it can become very time-consuming to attempt to deal with all enquiries on the phone. It can be very difficult to remember to tell callers all you would wish in order to convey the quality of your nursery. If callers insist on information over the phone, it is possible that it is the information which interests them rather than the nursery. It is preferable to make an appointment to discuss the nursery with prospective clients or send them an information brochure through the post.

The *brochure* is your second contact with the parents. This brochure should endeavour to portray the aspects of the nursery which you consider important. If it dwells on money and methods of payment that might be considered to be your priority, while if you focus on the children and the environment then parents may feel your heart is in the right place! A map will help parents find you on the first visit and a plan of the building will help them to know what to expect.

The following are two sample letters giving information about a nursery. While both of these letters are friendly, the difference between the two illustrates the importance of the right approach.

Figure 9: Sample Information Letters

Letter 1:
Kinder Minder Ltd
12 The Hill
Hilliton
West Ext 1234

Date

Dear Parent,

Thank you for your enquiry about *Kinder Minder*.

In this letter I will try to tell you a little about what we can offer you and your child. And because we believe that your child ought to feel as happy at *Kinder Minder* as at home, we'd like to welcome you to visit us and experience the atmosphere for yourself.

Most experts now agree that the early years are among the most important in a child's life and at *Kinder Minder* we make every effort to provide the stimulation and security that young children need. Ours is an informal environment where each child has the opportunity to develop social skills and for the children *Kinder Minder* is a fun place to be!

We have two large rooms - one, where the children eat, which doubles as a 'messy' room for painting, indoor sand play and other creative endeavours! Our second large room is fully carpeted with a fireplace, blackboard, Quadro climbing frame and all sorts of toys, games and books.

Kinder Minder is situated in a quiet cul-de-sac with a walled garden which is well equipped with climbing frame, sand-pit, playhouse etc.

Kinder Minder also provides a Montessori school for the benefit of nursery children (although we accept non-nursery children, where space permits). The Montessori school is supervised by a trained Montessori teacher and is fully equipped with a large range of Montessori teaching aids. There is, of course, a low pupil/teacher ratio in our Montessori.

At *Kinder Minder*, we strive to create a family atmosphere and a mix of children of all ages helps to contribute to the socialisation process. However, the nursery takes a maximum of 25 children, and has a full time staff of five.

As in most families, we have a number of guidelines so that both staff and children have clear guidelines to their behaviour. Some of these are:

*   That *Kinder Minder* is the children's place and must be kept safe, clean and interesting.
*   That touch is one of the most important things in a child's world.
*   That violence and all violent stories and activities should be discouraged.
*   That the children should not be punished by smacking.
*   That the children take priority and their needs take precedence over telephone calls and visitors.

I hope this gives you some idea of what you can expect from us for your child and we hope that you will decide that we can provide what you're looking for.

Appended to this letter is a plan of the area and the school.

Relevant fees can be discussed when you visit *Kinder Minder*.

I look forward to your child having a long and happy stay with us.

Sincerely,

Sandy Pitman.

Letter 2:
Kinder Minder Ltd
12 The Hill
Hilliton
West Ext 1234

Date

Dear Parents,

I would like to take this opportunity to welcome your child to *Kinder Minder*'s Montessori and day nursery.

Kinder Minder will be open from 8.00 to 6.30 from Monday to Friday.

* The nursery will include Montessori class   @ £58.00
  Nursery school fees will be paid on the **first day of each week**
* The Montessori class will be from 9-30 to 12-30
  There will be three Montessori terms:
  Term 1 - Sept, Oct, Nov and Dec   @ £228.00
  Term 2 - Jan, Feb, Mar and April   @ £228.00
  Term 3 - May, June, July and Aug   @ £199.00
  Montessori fees will be paid on the **first day of each term**

Kinder Minder will be closed for two weeks in August plus two other weeks in the year. All holidays have been accounted for in the fees.

Due to there being two staff I unfortunately will not be in a position to take on the extra administration involved in late payments and would appreciate your cooperation. We offer a 10% reduction in the case of two or more members of the same family attending the nursery school.

I hope you will try to become involved in every aspect of *Kinder Minder* and we hope to have activities etc in which we hope for parent participation ... more about that later.

I hope your child has a long and happy stay at the new *Kinder Minder*.

With Best wishes for the future,

_____

Chapter Thirteen
Parents, the Nursery and You

Meeting the Parents

It is worth remembering that the main ingredient in your business is *you*. It is you who can make it a success. In a service industry, as a nursery is, you are the main reason for your own success or failure.

Failure to give a good service is the downfall of many businesses. Providing a service is very different to selling a product. A product can be held, weighed, measured, compared for price and value and the results of its use can be judged. Product samples can be tasted in the supermarket. Service on the other hand is not quantifiable. It is different to different people. People's view of your service is personal and subjective.

Being in business, you must aim to give the customers what they want. Some parents' expectations will be too high and you will not be able to satisfy them, you can only do your best. You must be confident that the service you are giving is good and to the best of your ability. It is your chosen career to give a service and you should take pride in *your* job. You will find that some people may equate service with servility. You are not a servant: *you* determine the level of service, not the client.

Good service is based on good presentation and good communication. Here are a few pointers to your meeting with parents:

*   Smile and be relaxed. Avoid arranging to meet clients at a time when you are usually busy.
*   Look at the parents when you shake their hands. Remember also to look at the child, but resist any attempt to approach the child too soon.
*   Use the parents' and child's names and address relevant questions to a child who is old enough to understand.
*   You should try to dress casually and cheerfully while at the same time looking well groomed and responsible. Your clothes can inspire confidence in you. Although a uniform may denote a certain competence to the adults, to the children it can be a symbol of authority and may make them ill at ease with you.

The parents' most important impression will be gained when they visit the nursery. It is preferable that the visit is by appointment. While most days in the nursery will be calm and controlled it seems to be a law of nature that someone will choose to visit unexpectedly the day you are having trouble settling a new child. As we all know it only takes one note of discord to tempt most of the younger members to try out their lungs also! It can be quite a challenge to contrive some activity which will have the group enthralled for long enough to forget their ambitions to be Michael Jackson! Other times you may simply be involved in a story or some group activity and it may not be a convenient time for visitors. Children cannot be expected to concentrate on activities if they are constantly interrupted by your coming and going and it is unfair to the children and staff to be constantly interrupted by callers.

Appointments should be arranged so as to avoid times when the children will be expecting your undivided attention. The afternoon may be more organised and therefore may be a better time to arrange meetings with visitors. If someone calls without an appointment and at an inconvenient time offer them a brochure and arrange an appointment. They may possibly feel annoyed at having come to see you only to be sent away but it is better to risk annoying prospective clients than unsettling the nursery.

The visitors should be invited to take a leisurely stroll around the nursery. If you do offer them a cup of tea or coffee be sure they are not near the children. Visitors are often not sufficiently aware of the danger of spilling hot drinks on children. It is recommended that the parents have an opportunity to talk to you away from the hurly-burly of nursery activity. At this interview the parents may have many questions. You may give them a copy of the *Policies and procedures*, the *Parents' agreement*, *Booking form* etc. These documents should answer most of their questions. Invite them to take these home and study them before booking and if they have any questions to contact you.

When parents wish to reserve a place in the nursery it is normal practice to pay a booking fee. This can be a non-refundable deposit and/or the first week's fees in advance. Parents should specify the week in which their child will be starting, otherwise you may find you are holding a place for a number of weeks which you could otherwise have filled.

Parents' Involvement

Parents should be encouraged to help their child settle into the nursery. This can be done by visiting the nursery in the week before the child is due to start. This week can be counted as the child's settling-in week and it is best not to charge fees for this week. During the settling-in week the child and one parent should visit the nursery every day. The parent can leave the child for gradually increasing lengths of time. On the first day, for instance, the visit may be for one hour with the parent, on the second day the parent might stay a short time and then leave the child for a short while.

It must be impressed on the parents that when they leave children to the nursery they must not sneak out. Parents who sneak out might save themselves the pain of seeing their child upset, but they can lose their child's confidence. How would you feel if you went with a friend to a giant's party at which you knew nobody and just as you had found where the drinks were, she sneaked out and left you? I don't think I'd trust her with the car keys the next time!

The purpose of the settling-in week is for the child to get to know the carers and build up confidence in them. The child will be able to observe the other children and carers from her parent's side, venturing away when s/he feels confident to do so. It is important that the parent does not become involved in playing. If she does, the child will expect this to happen always and will not be very happy when mother or father leave to go to work. The parent should sit to one side of the room away from the play area and let the child leave and return to her side as the child wishes. As the child's confidence develops in a day or two, the parent can gradually wean herself away, perhaps starting by sitting in the next room, even with the door open. If the child wishes to remain with her s/he may be attracted to the playroom by the activities of the other children. The key to successful settling-in is gentleness.

At the end of a week of familiarising the child with the nursery, s/he may be ready to be left for most of the day. This decision must be taken by both the carer and the parent. You must not coerce the parent into leaving the child as she should feel comfortable with her decision. She may be reluctant and in that case you will need to reassure her that the child is ready for the break. Having spent some time with you, the child will be familiar with the nursery and, while s/he will no doubt miss her/his parents, will not feel s/he is among strangers. The parents must understand that the child is your first priority and that having left, they must be contactable and available to reassure their child if required.

Children and Nursery Staff

Especially in their first weeks, it is common for children to develop a relation with one particular member of staff. This is fine and once children feel comfortable with one member of staff they will be ready to get to know the other staff. Some staff may find it difficult to relax with the children while a parent is in the room. But when they experience how much easier it is on the child and ultimately the nursery when the children are confident, the staff will see the value of trying to be less self-conscious.

All staff have different personalities and different ways of relating to the children. It is unavoidable for individual staff to build up a stronger relationship with some children than with others, however it is inexcusable to treat any child more liberally out of favouritism. Staff must acknowledge to one another if they feel they have a tendency to favour one child over another. All staff, once they are aware, can then prevent any child being favoured or ignored.

Policies and Procedures

The policies and procedures of the nursery must be agreed with parents before they can make an informed commitment to the nursery. Depending on how you feel this may be done verbally or in writing.

Formal policies and procedures are designed to diminish the likelihood of misunderstandings between parents and management. It is desirable that parents know exactly what to expect from the nursery. As in any relationship, the majority of nursery-parent problems stem from misunderstandings. It is possible to reduce the risk of misunderstandings by being clear from the outset what type of service you are offering. The nursery-parent relationship is both a personal and a business relationship. One cannot always anticipate problems in a personal relationship but one can, to a great extent, anticipate and eliminate problems of a business nature.

When the parents visit the nursery, it is a good idea to first show them around and then, in the office, outline to them the policies and procedures. The parents will appreciate knowing exactly where they stand though they may be alarmed if it is put to them in too legalistic a form. For most parents your relationship is first and foremost a personal one based on trust, and only secondly a business relationship.

Policies and procedures should include:

1 Opening hours.
Will there be a late collection charge? Any charge for late collection should be large enough to compensate staff for overtime.

2 Days on which the nursery will be closed.
Bank holidays? Summer holidays?

3 Outline of amount of fees and when they are due.
Will fees be paid weekly? Monthly? In advance? Will fees be paid when parents take holidays or sick days from work? Some parents may have very generous holidays. Can your nursery afford to have reduced attendances? Parents generally are paid while on holidays.

4 Conditions (if any) under which reduced or no fees will be paid.
Eg Second child reductions? Absenteeism due to illness.

5 Nursery's policy on children bringing sweets, toys, books, etc to the nursery. It may be important for individual children to have a security toy or blanket. These should generally be allowed and a child should not be expected to share, but personal toys can lead to fighting. Many parents feel strongly that sweets should not be freely available in the nursery. It is normal for children to have nursery parties etc. It should be explained to parents that while these occasions are rare, no child should be forbidden from sharing in the treats as this will cause the child to feel excluded from the group. In the case of allergies or special dietary needs (such as vegetarian) substitute treats should be supplied.

6 Daily routine.

7 Children's menu.
Will food exceptions be made for individual children on the grounds of religion, allergies or vegetarianism?

8 Parent access to the nursery.
Parents should be permitted free access to all parts of the nursery when their child is in attendance.

9 Religious ethos of the nursery.
This should be clearly spelled out. If there is a religious ethos in the nursery, it should be remembered that while many of the children may be predominantly from one religion, other children may belong to other religious traditions, or come from non-religious families. It may be preferable to confine religious activities to non-exclusive prayers, songs etc.

10 Parents must establish that the child is under supervision before

notice of removal from creche.

the parents leave the premises. It is not recommended that children be collected by a person unknown to the nursery staff without prior arrangement. Children should be collected from the nursery only by the parents or by someone authorised by them to do so and by prior arrangement with the nursery staff.

11 Sick children should not be brought to the nursery.
Children who have been absent through illness should not be readmitted without a doctor's certificate indicating that the child is no longer contagious. (Parents should appreciate that, though they may be reluctant to comply, their child will benefit from the strict enforcement of this requirement.)

12 The nursery insurance cover
This should be clearly described.

Parents' Agreement

It is also recommended that parents sign an Agreement or Contract with the nursery. This covers the nursery in very unusual events such as a parent refusing to pay outstanding fees, etc. The conditions of this Agreement provide protection for both the parents and the nursery.

You may explain to parents that in order to ensure that you can provide the quality service that their children are entitled to, it is essential that the financial status of the nursery is stable and that salaries and overheads cannot be reduced because of absentee losses in income. In essence, this agreement is a guarantee to the nursery that the parents will financially support the booking which you in turn guarantee to their child.

Figure 10: Sample Parents' Agreement

I agree to;

1. Pay a booking fee, or first week's fees at the time of booking and indicate the date of commencement and termination of registration.

2. Pay weekly/monthly* the full nursery fee. A late charge of £__.__ per day may be added to fees not paid.

3. Pay Montessori or swimming fees as required (specify period).

4. The usual annual holiday period is two weeks. If my child is to be absent for more than two weeks I agree to pay the fees in advance. If this fee is not paid in advance I understand my child may be disenrolled, with re-enrollment depending on availability of space and payment of fees.

5. In case of withdrawal of my child from the nursery I agree to give one week's notice or pay one week's fees.

6. In cases of minor illness the nursery has my permission to administer as it sees fit for my child's best interests.

7. I have read and understand the Policies and Procedures Agreement and agree to carry out the parents' responsibilities under same.

8. Should the supervisor of the nursery determine that my child is not adapting to the nursery programme or that I have not fully carried out this contract, my child will be withdrawn from the nursery after two weeks' notice and this agreement terminated.

9. This contract is subject to change with one month's notice.

Parents' Signatures   _____

_____

Child/ren's name/s   _____

_____

Date   _____

Children's Personal Details

It is important that the nursery has contact phone numbers and a brief medical history for each child. This should be filled in on a *Child's Record Card*. Be sure that you have at least two contact phone numbers especially if both parents work together.

Discuss with parents if there have been any changes in the child's recent past which may cause the child to have problems settling in to the nursery. The sort of events which could inhibit a child from settling include:

* The birth of a new baby.
* Moving house.
* Death of a person known to the child or a pet.
* Parents' divorce or separation.
* Difficulty with past child-minder, Au-pair or unsettling experience in a playgroup, other nursery or any group of children.

It may be helpful to know how many children are in the family and the child's position in the family.

Figure 11: Child's Record Card

CONFIDENTIAL
Please Complete All Questions

Child's Name _____

Date Of Birth   Day: _____ Month: _____ Year: 19_____

Address _____

_____

_____ Home phone number _____

Family Doctor _____ Phone number _____
*Mother's Name _____
Mother's daytime phone number _____
*Father's Name _____
Father's daytime phone number _____
*Or carer as appropriate

Has the above named child been immunised against:
Polio   yes/no
Mumps, Measles, Rubella (MMR)   yes/no
Diptheria, Tetanus, Whooping cough (3 in 1)   yes/no
Tuberculosis (BCG)   yes/no

Has the above named child any:
Allergies?   yes*/no
Physical abnormality?   yes*/no
Sight, hearing, or speech defects?   yes*/no
* If 'yes' please give details _____

_____

Any other relevant information:

_____

Type of booking:
Full day _____ Mornings only _____ Afternoons only _____
Mon _____ Tues _____ Wed _____ Thurs _____ Fri _____
Anticipated Booking Period   From: _____ To: _____

SIGNED _____
Relationship to child _____

Figure 12: Sample Daily Routine

8.15 NURSERY OPENS

8.15-9.30

Arrival of children and free play. The children choose their own activity from the range of equipment and are encouraged to mix with the other children. This helps to develop their social skills.

9.30-10.30

Montessori class begins for older children. Stimulating activities are made available in the activity room for the younger children under the supervision of the playgroup leader. This includes playdough, drawing, painting, sand, construction toys, etc.

10.30-10.45

Break time. Fruit juice or milk, crackers, fruit, rusks etc.

10.45-11.30

Creative play - music, dancing, singing or garden play.

11.30-12.00

Story time - conversation, rhymes, singing, ball or garden play, tidy up and prepare for lunch.

12.00

Lunch. A hot nourishing meal. The menu is changed daily, and fresh unprocessed food is used as much as possible. Details of food supplied are posted daily on the menu board in the dining room.

Half day children leave.

AFTERNOON

1.00-2.00

Quiet activities. Children are encouraged to spend time in quiet activities such as reading, resting, listening to taped music or stories.

2.00-2.45

"Up time". Children have free play and afternoon children arrive.

2.45-3.30

Younger children who may be resting are awoken. Older children go for a walk, have outdoor play (weather permitting), or organised group activity.

3.45-5.00

In the afternoon the children are more tired and less likely to enjoy participating in structured play. They are encouraged to choose their own activity and therefore activities are more spontaneous.

5.00-5.30

Free play and departure.

5.30-6.00

Children and staff join in a general tidy up eg hoovering, dusting etc.

NURSERY CLOSES.

Chapter Fourteen
Staff

The staff are a very important element in the environment of the day nursery. It is not only important that your staff are well trained but also that you like them, and that you will work together as a team.

The number of people you should employ and the qualifications that they should have depend on the age range and number of children in your nursery. If you have a mixed age range you will need a mix of staff with nursery and teaching qualifications. The age range of your children will be dictated by the type of building in which you operate and by the requirements of your clientele. (*See Chapter Two*.) Unless you are catering specifically for children with special needs or illnesses the majority of the staff should have a child-centred qualification rather than a medical one.

Many areas will have standards set by the local authority which will determine the child/staff ratio in your nursery. In Ireland these standards are set by the Health Boards. In addition to local guidelines, your insurance policy may also set a child/staff ratio above which you must not operate. In general, it is desirable to keep the child/staff ratio as low as possible.

You might wish to employ someone who does not have a formal qualification but who has experience and is a 'natural' with children. Experience in child care is indeed a very important 'qualification'. Experienced people without formal training should be encouraged to take a part-time course while continuing to work. This will also enhance their potential for promotion within your staff structure. The following is a short list of the formal qualifications which are currently offered in Ireland and the UK.

* Nursery nurse qualification offered by State funded and independent Colleges.
* Children's nurse (RSCN).
* Diploma in Child care.
* National Nursery Examination Board (NNEB).
* Child care certificate.
* (Irish) Pre-school playgroup certificate.
* Montessori diploma.

Recruitment

There are a number of ways of recruiting staff, for instance by advertising in newspapers, in training centres and in employment exchanges.

Newspaper advertising has a large circulation and you are sure to get a large number of replies. You may get a large number of unsuitable replies unless your advertisement is very detailed and specific. Normally, newspaper advertising is recommended if you are looking for experienced staff who may be already employed. As with all newspaper advertising the disadvantage is the expense of the advertisement. Advertising in Nursery and Montessori periodicals will reach a large readership.

If experience is not the main criterion but a specified qualification is, then it is better to target your recruitment campaign by advertising in the training centres. These advertisements are usually free and most good training centres run a placement service for their trainees. The applicant may not normally have extensive experience but most good training centres seek to arrange in-course hands-on experience for their students. You can offer your nursery to be considered for training: you should take note of any students who particularly impress you with a view to considering them for future job vacancies.

There is normally no charge for advertising in the National Employment Exchange. Information on job creation incentive schemes can also be obtained from your local Employment Exchange and is well worth investigating.

Wages

Unfortunately wages in child care do not reflect the level of responsibility which the job demands. This is not only true of the private sector but is also the situation in the Social Services sector. What a nursery can afford to pay is directly linked to the income of the clients and any other funding the nursery may receive. Women's pay tends to be low despite Equal Pay legislation and it can become nonviable for a woman to work if child care becomes too expensive. It is recommended that child care employers pay a reasonable wage to all employees. At the same time the following points must be considered:

* You must determine how much your nursery can afford to pay your staff.

* The fees you charge must reflect the qualifications and thus the wages of your staff.
* Ask prospective employees how much they expect to be paid, this will help you to judge whether you can afford this employee. If you can only pay a sum which is well below someone's expectations they will only stay until they can get a better paid position.

It is important to have a contented staff. Discontented staff will find it difficult to enjoy their work and it will be the children who will suffer in the long run. Remember the child care business is unlike most businesses in that you are dealing with a customer who is a child, and it is in their interests that you be very aware of your staff's needs.

Staff must have some procedure by which their grievances can be heard. Staff might find it easier to talk over problems with the supervisor rather than the employer if these are two separate functions . The supervisor will then try to sort it out with the employer. All the staff should have regular meetings at which they will discuss problems or progress with the children or parents and staff problems. These meetings could be an informal chat over coffee or a structured meeting on a weekly or monthly basis scheduled for after the nursery closes.

Employees should have a clear idea what is expected of them. This can form part of their employment contract. Their job description should include a description of the daily staff and children's routine and as such should be more detailed than the daily routine given to parents. If you have any strong opinions about the way the nursery is to operate, be sure new staff are aware of your views. For example do you read any stories or do you edit or ban very violent stories? Do you permit smoking among staff? You cannot expect staff to know what you want unless you tell them.

It is important that whatever type of contract you have with your employees it is operated on the basis of goodwill. In a day nursery it is difficult to specifically demarcate each person's total job because the staff must work as a team. For example, while one person may have specific responsibility for the three to four year-olds, that is not to preclude her from helping with babies if the need arises. Likewise the babies' nurse may perhaps like to spend some time reading to older children. The nursery staff should work with and help one another so that the nursery runs smoothly at all times.

Interviewing

It is not unusual to receive a great number of replies to an advertisement for a position caring for children. Some people feel that it is an easy job which anyone can do if they have babysat or have younger brothers or sisters. To avoid having to spend an inordinate number of hours or days interviewing, you should try to short-list applicants before the actual interview.

The first contact with the applicant may be on the phone. Before you advertise you must decide what type of person you are looking for and have relevant questions prepared to ask over the phone. For example, if you only want someone with a specific qualification then your first question should establish whether the applicant has the necessary qualification. If you also feel that experience is required, that could be addressed in the next question. Having responded favourably to three of four very specific questions, the applicant might be invited to submit a Curriculum Vitae.

It is recommended that you reply to all applicants who submit a CV if possible, and candidates who are interviewed will expect to be informed whether or not they have been successful.

Job applicants' CVs can tell a lot about the person. The CV should have the qualities which you will require in the candidate:

*   The CV should be neat and clearly written. If the person considers the job worth having she should be willing to spend some time and perhaps money on a professionally presented CV.
*   The CV should not be untidily folded and squashed into an envelope. If the applicant is serious about her application for the position you are offering she should treat her CV as a serious application and send it preferably unfolded in a large envelope.
*   The CV should contain all the applicant's work history, with no gaps.

Before interviewing make notes of anything arising out of the CV which you would particularly want explained. When the candidate leaves the interview, make a few quick notes of your immediate impressions. It is surprising how confused you can become after only a few interviews!

If possible try not to interview on your own, a second opinion can be very helpful.

Employees can be given a *Contract of Employment* as well as a job description. While this contract can be very basic and cover only such things as wages and hours of work, you might decide to have a much more detailed contract due to the nature of this work.

Figure 13: Contract of Employment

Personal details
Date _____
Employee's name _____
Address _____
_____

Phone Number _____

Employment
Date of commencement of employment _____
History of any previous service which counts as part of your
continuous employment _____
Annual salary £ _____
You will be paid weekly/monthly in arrears.
Deductions which will be made are: _____
_____

Position or Job title
You will be employed for a probationary period of:

Normal working hours
 Monday:
 Tuesday:
 Wednesday:
 Thursday:
 Friday:
 Saturday:
 Sunday:
Total no. of working days per week/month _____

Holiday entitlement
 Public Holidays
 Other

Conditions pertaining to sick leave
For instance will full pay be given? Will a doctor's certificate be
required if employee is to qualify for payment during sick leave?
Will a doctor's certificate be required before staff can return to
work after sickness to prevent staff from infecting children?

Discipline

If you have a grievance you are advised to contact: _____
(In some cases this might be a Board of Management or Committee.)

Discipline measures may be taken in the following types of situation:

Examples:

Inability to work in harmony with other staff.

Job incompetence.

Conduct prejudicial to the reputation of the nursery, its management and/or other staff.

Unreliability in punctuality and attendance.

Disciplinary procedure:

a Initial oral warning

b Followed by two written warnings

c If a resolution cannot be found, dismissal will be necessary.

Termination of employment will be with the following notice:

By employee

By employer

Employed less than 2 years: 2 weeks

Employed more than 2 years: 4 weeks

Summary dismissal without notice may occur for the following reasons:

Examples:

Gross cruelty to children.

Drunkenness.

Theft.

Signed

By Employer _____

By Employee _____

Note: *No employee's rights in law may be negated by signing a contract of employment.*

Staff and their Children in the Nursery

For a member of staff to have her own child in the nursery has many obvious advantages but it is not without its problems. There are many types of problems which can arise and it seems that no matter what the mother does to prevent them arising she will still run the risk of encountering one or a combination of them.

There may be jealousy problems, the child may become jealous of the time the mother spends with the other children or the other children may become jealous of the time she spends with her own child. In trying to avoid overindulging her own child, the mother risks tending towards the other extreme and ignoring her child. This can result in the child feeling very rejected. On the other hand, she might spend more time with her child than any other and the other children and staff may resent this. It is very difficult to reach a happy medium!

In discipline, too, the same types of problems can arise. The mother might be overly permissive with her child or she may be overly strict.

The other nursery staff may also have difficulties with this situation. For example they may feel, rightly or wrongly, that they are unable to discipline a child whose mother works in the nursery, or the mother may intervene. They may not feel that they are able to build up a normal carer-child relationship with the child as the child's own mother is there.

It is very important for the mother and the other members of staff to consider the problems very carefully before coming to a final decision. Placing a child in a nursery is a difficult decision for any mother but perhaps even more difficult for someone working in a nursery. Working in a nursery can cause the mother to have higher expectations of her child's nursery. But in the long run, while every child will benefit from quality day care, the mother's relationship with her child could be harmed by the conflict of interests which may arise if the child is with the mother in the day nursery.

The Trainee in the Nursery

It is the policy of many good training centres to place students in nurseries so that the student may gain practical experience while studying. Some centres prefer to place students for 'block' periods of six or eight weeks during the academic year, while others place their students for two or three days each week throughout the year. It is preferable for students to spend an extended period in the nursery so that they can become familiar with the nursery. Students will get greater benefit from the experience if they are given time to become familiar with the nursery staff and their routine and to build up a relationship with the children.

It is not in the children's interests to have a large proportion of students among the staff. If there is a large number of untrained staff this could lead to accidents due to the students' lack of experience. The children can also become insecure if, due to the lack of permanent staff, they have to make a number of temporary attachments due to frequent personnel changes as students come and go. One student per three full-time staff is usually manageable, and with this type of ratio the children will not become too dependent on the student relationships.

The nursery can gain more than just another pair of hands by facilitating trainee child care workers. By participating in training schemes, the nursery is helping to guarantee that there is a pool of highly qualified and experienced staff available. The nursery which takes satisfaction in preparing students will help to maintain a pool of high quality child care personnel and will therefore enhance the quality of day care in general. The student who is helped and encouraged will become happy and relaxed and will help the children to feel more relaxed in her company.

At the beginning of each year or term, the nursery manager should confirm with the training centres the dates when they will be requiring the nursery to take on a student placement. This will enable the nursery to plan in advance, and reduces the likelihood of the nursery being inundated with students in one particular period while having no students at another time.

When the student arrives introduce her to all the members of staff and give her an outline of the daily routine for both children and staff.

Give the student time to observe and build up confidence in the children and in herself. The student should not be expected to organise an activity or group until she feels ready to do so.

If there are particular 'do's and don'ts' in the nursery, be sure to tell the student. Not all nurseries are alike and so the student cannot be expected to know the ethos automatically. For example, some nurseries may permit the children to have snacks whenever they wish, while others may not. Some may permit staff to receive personal phone calls, others may not.

Invite the student to become involved in preparing activities for the children. For instance, tell the student where the painting materials are kept, how you make up paints, how much the children should be involved in setting up and tidying up, and so on. The students should be encouraged to become involved and not to sit to one side taking notes! Students should aim to get as much practical experience as possible.

As the student becomes more familiar with the children she

should be encouraged to organise an activity for a small group of children. This is not an opportunity for other staff to take a break and let the student take the full group. It can be very disconcerting for a student to be left to organise ten reluctant children to hear a story! The other members of staff should remain close at hand while the student is presenting an activity to four or five children who should be 'hand picked' for their cooperative nature!

The student should develop while on placement. The manager of the nursery should understand the course which the student is taking. It is usual for the nursery manager to complete an assessment of students and it is recommended that she retain a copy for her records. It is possible that a student may return at some later stage for a position and it is surprising how much one can forget about any particular student after a number of years.

Appendix 1
Healthy Eating Every Day

Extracted from: *Food and Drink For Under Fives* The London Food Commission

DIETARY GUIDELINES

While the following guidelines are very helpful, it is recommended that nursery managers also check the latest guidelines from their local Health Centre or Council.

A. Children under one year old

Infant feeding: Nothing can match breast milk, which provides both good nourishment and some of the mother's immunity to diseases. Ideally, all babies should be breastfed or fed on expressed human milk for the first few months. If breastfeeding is not possible then modified infant formulae are available.

No cereals or thickeners should be put in the bottle unless medically prescribed, as they can alter the nutrient balance of the feed and artificially satisfy the baby's hunger.

Weaning: The best foods to introduce to a baby are pureed cooked vegetables, fruit, potatoes and other starchy vegetables and ground cereals such as rice or fine cornmeal made into a porridge.

These first solids are usually introduced between three months and six months, depending how hungry the baby is. They should be given to the baby on a spoon.

As the baby's appetite grows so can the range of foods. As chewing starts the texture can become coarser and by one year old the child should be eating the same types of food as the older children (and the staff) in the centre.

Milk: Whether a child is breast or bottle fed with a formula feed, no other type of milk should be introduced until the child is at least six months old. At this stage cow's milk can be given. Concern about the role of saturated fats, such as that in milk, has lead some people to give skimmed milk to babies. Neither the DHSS (Department of Health and Social Services, UK) nor the American Medical Association currently recommend skimmed or semi-skimmed milk for babies and young infants. If the child is not given full-fat milk then care must be taken to ensure that the calories and nutrients they would have obtained in the milk are made up through other foods.

Salt: It has long been known that babies' kidneys are unable to cope with too much salt. No salt should be added to weaning foods during their preparation and cooking.

Spices: Most spices and herbs are well tolerated in weaning foods, but chillis and chilli powder can upset young children.

Sugar: Babies have no need for sugar. Giving it will only encourage a 'sweet tooth' and give the baby calories without nutrients - empty calories. Sugar should not be added to weaning foods during their preparation and cooking.

Dietary Fibre: Little research has been done on the effects of giving young children diets in which cereals are mainly unrefined, for example wholemeal bread, wholemeal flour, brown rice and brown pasta. A rapid increase in the fibre content of the diet is not advised as it takes time for the gut to adapt and rapid, frequent bowel movements may result.

A mixture of refined and unrefined starchy foods - such as mixing wholemeal with white flour, wholemeal bread and white rice and pasta, and so forth - may be a suitable compromise until further evidence is available.

Pulses and Dahls (Split Pulses): Dahls can be introduced as a weaning food from about four months as long as the dahl is smooth. Well-cooked small beans such as mung and aduki beans are suitable from about 9 months and whole larger beans such as well-cooked kidney beans and chickpeas can be introduced a few months later.

Vitamins: Most children eating a well-balanced varied diet will not need vitamin supplements. (However, the DHSS advises that all children under the age of 2 years and preferably until 5 years should receive special supplements of vitamins A,C, and D in the form of drops which are available from the local child health clinic or health visitors)

B. Children one to five years old

Milk: Milk provides many useful nutrients. An average of a pint a day is usually recommended for children under five. Not more than 1.75 pints is advised as it can limit the appetite for other essential foods.

There is a major debate about the type of milk children under five should be drinking - skimmed or full-fat. The DHSS *Report on Diet and Cardiovascular Disease* says their recommendation to reduce the saturated fat in the diet "is not intended for infants; or or for children under the age of five who usually obtain a substantial proportion of their dietary energy from cow's milk" and that families opting for skimmed or semi-skimmed milk should "continue to provide whole cow's milk for children below the age of five". The reasons for this are not given, but they are assumed to stem from concern that if the milk fat is removed from the child's diet then undernutrition might result.

At the same time there is growing evidence that fat in the diet in childhood is related to heart disease in later life, and that saturated fats in particular are responsible. Full-fat milk is a major source of saturated fats in many children's diets.

A strong body of opinion feels that if children have good appetites and eat a variety of nutritious foods that the type of milk they drink is immaterial to their current nutritional state and that they should be cutting down on the saturated fats as a protective measure for the future. In terms of calories, the difference between a pint of full-fat milk and a pint of skimmed milk is about 190 calories - equivalent to two medium slices of bread.

The debate is currently unresolved and work is being carried out to clarify the issues and study the evidence. If you feel uncertain about your own policy then contact your District Health Authority Dietetic Department, or the London Food Commission (UK), for further advice.

Fats: Both the DHSS and the Health Education Council advise a reduction in fat intake for the majority of the population as a protective measure against heart disease and obesity in particular. They do not say that this is necessarily recommended for children under five.

The strongest evidence relating fat intake to heart disease is for saturated fats. Cutting back dramatically on total fat may lead to problems in getting enough calories in the diet. It needs over twice as much bulky starch as fat to get the same amount of calories. It may be sensible, therefore, to put more emphasis on cutting down on the saturated fats rather than all fats. This can be achieved by reducing the amounts of fatty meats and meat products, butter, lard and hard margarine. More fish, pulses, lean meat and poultry, and margarines and oils based on corn, sunflower or soya can be used instead.

Sugar: There is little doubt that sugar intake in children is related to tooth decay. Sugar provides no nutrients other than calories, and it is often associated with fat in food - eg in cake and biscuits. Diets containing a lot of sugar may also be relatively low in vitamins and minerals.

Sugar itself is unnecessary as a source of energy. All starchy foods are digested to form glucose which is the body's main energy source. Brown sugar and honey, which are just as bad for the teeth, contain insignificant amounts of minerals.

Dietary Fibre: With less fat and sugar in the diet, the child is more likely to be eating starchy and bulky foods such as bread, potatoes, rice, pasta, fruit and vegetables. The child's stomach can fill up with this bulk and satisfy the appetite even though he or she hasn't actually had enough calories to last until the next main meal. In such circumstances, between-meal snacks such as fruit, dried fruit, sandwiches and the like, become increasingly important.

In a well-balanced diet with lots of starchy food, fruit and vegetables, the specially concentrated sources of fibre such as bran are not necessary and should not be given unless specifically prescribed.

Salt: By the time the child is over a year old there should be little risk of kidney damage from excess salt. However, current evidence suggests that there may be a link between high salt intake and high blood pressure in later life. It is sensible that children do not develop a taste for highly salted food and that little or no salt is used in preparing and cooking foods.

Nuts: It is generally recommended that young children should not be given nuts. There is a possible danger of choking and there are further complications from inhaling a piece of nut which do not result from inhaling other foods. Generally, once a child is able to chew and swallow all sorts of foods, say by the time they are three years old, then nuts should not present a problem, and indeed are a good source of unsaturated fats, protein and B vitamins. For younger children smooth peanut butter (and other nut pastes) are a useful alternative.

C. Additives

In addition to the dietary guidelines above, Government food regulations advise against certain additives in food meant specifically for babies and young children. Most food which children eat - whether crisps or orangeade, raisins or ice lollies - is not sold as being 'specifically for babies and young children' and so may contain these additives. If staff are in a position to check the ingredients of food and drinks, then the following additives (often known by their 'E' numbers) are to be avoided:

preservatives and antitoxidants: E250, E251, E310, E311, E312,
E320, E321 and ethoxyquin
2-aminoethanol
alpha-cellulose
sodium hydrogen L-glutamate
guanosine 5' - (disodium phosphate)
inosine 5' - (disodium phosphate)
polydextrose
sodium 5' - ribonucletide

Children with suspected food-related asthma, eczema, skin rashes or
hyperactivity should seek medical advice, and may be advised to
avoid the additives:

Colourings (azo dyes): E102, E104, E107, E110, E122, E123,
E124, E127, E128, E131, E132, E133, E142, E151, E155, E180,
and new coccine.

Preservatives (benzoates): E210, E211, E212, E213, E213,
E215, E216, E217, E218 and E219.

Appendix 2
Planning Applications - Sample Application

NB: These notes are specifically for Cork Corporation and are for sample purposes only. Anyone intending to apply for Planning Permission or Bye-Law Approval must contact their local Planning Authority.

1. Planning application may be made for any one of the following:-
   (a) Outline Permission means a permission for development which is granted subject to the subsequent approval by the Planning Authority of detailed plans. This does not permit the carrying out of any development.
   (b) Approval means (i) approval of detailed plans consequent on an outline permission or (ii) approval of details of a development which is required to be obtained under a condition attached to an earlier permission or approval.
   (c) Permission means "full" permission ie when detailed plans are lodged at the beginning.
   (d) Retention means permission to retain on land any structure or the continuance of any land use.
   An outline permission may not be made in respect of retention.

2. A valid Outline Application is as follows;-
   (a) Two copies of application form fully completed.
   (b) Two copies of site location map. (*see note 5*)
   (c) Full page of newspaper advertisement containing Notice of Intention or copy of site notice. (*see note 4*)
   (d) Appropriate Fee. (*see note 6*)

3. A valid application for approval, permission, retention is as follows;-
   (a) Three copies of application form fully completed.
   (b) Three copies of site location map. (*see note 3*)
   (c) Full page of newspaper advertisement containing Notice of Intention or copy of site notice. (*see note 4*)
   (d) Three copies of detailed drawing. (*see note 5*)
   (e) Appropriate Fee. (*see note 6*)

4. Notice of intention;-

(a) The application must be submitted within 14 days of the advertisement appearing in the press.

(b) The advertisement in a newspaper circulated in the area must contain:

(1) "Cork Corporation" or "Cork City" as a heading

(2) the name of the applicant

(3) The full address of the structure, or the location of the land, defined as exactly as possible. (District and Town Land names are not sufficient on their own.)

(4) the nature and extent of the development, or

(5) where the application relates to the retention of a structure, the nature of the proposed use of the structure and the period of the proposed retention or

(6) where the application relates to the continuance of any use, the nature of such use.

(7) a notice fixed on land or structure (site notice) must be made on durable material, fixed in a conspicuous position for at least one month and be capable of being read by a person using the public road. It must be headed 'Application to Planning Authority' and contain details similar to those mentioned in 4(b) above.

5. Plans, Drawings, and Site Map

Drawings of elevations and sections should be drawn to scale which should be indicated thereon and should indicate in figures the principal dimensions (including overall height of any proposed structure), and the distance of the structure from the boundaries of the site. Drawing related to reconstruction, alteration and extension should be marked or coloured to distinguish between the existing structure and the work proposed.

An up to date Site Location Map of not less than 1:2500 should be used and show the scale, north-point, and outline of the site, adjacent roads and buildings and other significant landmarks.

6. Fees for Planning Applications

The fee which must be lodged with each planning application is as follows:

Dwellings £32 per dwelling
Domestic Extensions and other improvements £16 per dwelling
All other buildings £1.75 per sq. metre of gross floor space

Enquiries concerning fee for developments other than those listed above should be made to the Planning Authority.

7. Consultations
    Prior to submission of planning application consultations with the planning authority are recommended in order to ensure that the application will be in conformity with the Authority's policies and objectives and minimise the possibility of the application being found to be unacceptable.

8. Further information may be obtained from Planning Department, Cork Corporation, Abbeycourt House, George's Quay, Cork Tel; (021) 966222

July 1989

Appendix 3
Minimum Legal Requirements and Standards for Day Care Services for Children

Extracts of recommendations from the *Minimum Legal Requirements and Standards for Daycare Services for Children: Report of a Committe Appointed by the Minister for Health* Ireland, May 1985.

5.1

The Children (Care and Protection) Bill provides that health boards will act as local registration authorities for day care services. Any person, therefore, providing or proposing to provide a child-minding service, a sessional service or a full-day service will be required to apply for registration to the local health board.

On receipt of an application the health board should arrange for an officer to visit the applicant and the premises for the purpose of preparing a report.

5.2

In order to qualify for registration, certain requirements should be satisfied as to:

a   suitability of the applicant;
b   suitability of the premises;
c   equipment and facilities;
d   insurance cover;
e   adult/child ratio, age group, etc;
f   in the case of sessional services and full day services, training and qualifications of the applicant and/or staff; and
g   quality of the care being provided.

Factors to be taken into account under these headings are outlined in the remainder of this chapter.

5.3 Suitability of the Applicant etc.

Before granting registration the health board should satisfy itself that the applicant or person employed by the applicant to work in the service being provided:

i   is of good character;
ii   Has the personal characteristics and skills required to relate well to children and their parents. (factors to be taken into account would include personality, enthusiasm, dedication and energy of the applicant and any staff;
iii   is free from any defect or disease which could endanger the health and well-being of the child. (Applicants and any staff should be required to undergo a routine medical examination and chest x-ray).
iv   has not been convicted of any serious offence eg fraud and in particular offences involving bodily injury or sexual abuse;
v   is not restricted from looking after foster children, running a day care service or working in residential child care.

Provisions (iii) (iv) and (v) should also apply to any person residing at the premises where the service is being or is intended to be provided.

5.4 Suitability of the Premises

A health board should ensure that the premises in which a service is to be provided:

i   is clean, well lit, ventilated and heated (minimum 18°c or 65°f.)
ii   has an adequate and safe water supply;
iii   has toilet and wash basin facilities;
iv   has adequate and hygienic kitchen arrangements;
v   does not constitute a fire or health hazard;
vi   is of adequate size.
A minimum of 2.32 sq mtrs (25 sq ft) of floor space per child is desirable. Hallways etc are not to be included in the calculation of space available to children. An outdoor play area is desirable in all cases but should be essential in the case of full day services.

5.5   Equipment and Facilities

All day care services should have adequate provision for:

i   rest eg cots.
ii   play (suitable toys and equipment).

iii   safety (for example first aid box, safety gates, stair guards, fire precautions).

5.6   Insurance

The possession of adequate insurance cover should be an essential requirement for registration. The insurance policy obtained should at least cover the following areas:

i   Public Liability; (to include provision for outings, where applicable;

ii   Employers Liability if there is any other person employed; (to include provision for volunteers, trainees etc. where applicable);

iii   Theft and fire.

We would draw attention to the fact that service providers under the age of majority, 18 years, should ensure that their age does not preclude them from cover under their insurance contracts.

Individual providers are in the best position to determine the type and extent of insurance most suited to their needs. If it is intended to undertake any extra activities (eg outings for children) the insurers of the service should be notified and any additional cover necessary obtained in good time. In particular it may be necessary to obtain extra motor insurance cover for staff, volunteers, trainees and others involved in such activities.

5.7   Adult/Child Ratios

The maximum number of children who may be catered for depends on a number of factors, particularly the age of the children involved and the type of service being provided.

5.7.3   Adult/Child ratios - Full-Day Services

The aim should be to have an adult/child ratio of one to six subject to the following:

i   Where the children are under one year of age there should be an adult/child ratio of 1-3.

ii   Where the children are aged between one and two and a half years there should be an adult/child ratio of one to five.

iii   Untrained staff (i.e. cooks, cleaners etc.) are to be excluded from the calculation of adult/child ratios.

We are conscious of the fact that many existing services operate on a ration of one to eight or more children and that sudden enforcement of an average ratio of one to six might lead to a disruption of these services. Consequently we recommend that an adult/child ratio of one to eight is acceptable in the short term. The aim should be to reduce the ratios to the more intensive level of one to six within a reasonable period of time and this ratio should be made compulsory within two years of regulations being introduced.

In relation to the care of children under one year of age some members considered that an adult/child ratio of 1-1 would be necessary because of the special needs of this age group, in particular the complete dependence of such young children on their adult 'carers'.

While the entire committee agreed on the need for a very intensive adult/child ratio, other members considered that a 1-1 ratio would be too restrictive. An adult/child ratio of 1-2 or 1-3, while not being ideal, would be acceptable to those members provided that there is a limited overall number of children under one year of age catered for in full-day services. If significant numbers of such children were to avail of the service the staff would not be in a position to provide the intensive level of care necessary.

We therefore recommend that not more than 15% (ie approximately one out of every seven children) in full-day services should be under one year of age.

5.9   Special Requirements for Full-day Services

5.9.1   Qualifications of Staff and Supervision

If the person in charge of a full-day service is not qualified in child care, a suitable qualified member of staff should be appointed to act in a supervisory capacity.

Staff generally should have a relevant qualification. However persons who have a minimum of three years experience of working directly with children in a day care centre at the time the regulations are brought into effect, should be exempted from this requirement as a once-off arrangement. Our intention is to avoid a situation where staff who do not hold formal qualifications, but who are otherwise suitable and have appropriate experience, would no longer be allowed to provide a service.

Trainees should at all times be supervised by a qualified member of staff.

5.9.2   Activities and Group Size

Different rooms/areas should as far as practicable be reserved for different activities e.g. cooking, sleeping, etc. It is also important that attention should be paid to group size. Ideally children should be divided into small groups and children within these groups should preferably be of different ages and different stages of development.

Appendix 4
Suggested Layouts

Figure 14: Adapting premises

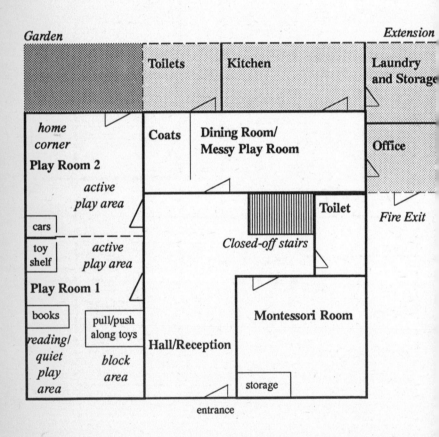

Garden · Extension · Toilets · Kitchen · Laundry and Storage · home corner · Play Room 2 · Coats · Dining Room/ Messy Play Room · Office · active play area · cars · Toilet · Fire Exit · toy shelf · active play area · Closed-off stairs · Play Room 1 · books · pull/push along toys · Montessori Room · reading/ quiet play area · Hall/Reception · block area · storage · entrance

Sample layout for adapting a typical private house for use as a 15 place day nursery

Figure 15: Purpose-built premises

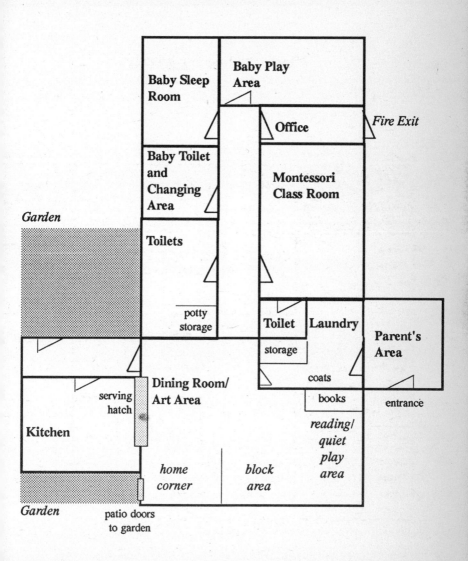

Sample layout for a purpose-built 25 place day nursery

Resources

Courses

Certificate in Pre-school Care
Dublin College of Catering
Cathal Brugha Street
Dublin 1
Tel (01) 747886
This is a two year NCEA qualification for pre-school and day nursery workers.

Academy of Childcare
44 Leeson Street Lower
Dublin
Tel (01) 601214 / 980753

The Montessori Education Centre
41/46 North Gt George's St
Dublin 1
Tel (01) 721581

Portobello School of Childcare
59 South Richmond St
Dublin 2
Tel (01) 755509

London Montessori Centre
12 Hume Street
Dublin 2
Tel (01) 767761/767730
Childcare (NNEB) and Montessori training

The VEC
Bull Alley, Liberties
Dublin 1
Tel (01) 540044
Child care course

School of Practical Childcare
Heronford Lane
Shankill
Co Dublin
Tel (01) 822625/977995
Day Nursery Management Course

Somers & Associates
42 Kincora Drive
Dublin 3
Tel (01) 331951
Day Nursery Management Course

Professional Education Association for Child Homecare (PAECH)
3 Gort na Mona Drive
Dublin 18
Tel (01) 855158
Childminders course

For advice and information on courses in the UK,
write to:
ECCTIS
PO Box 88
Walton Hall
Milton Keynes MK7 6DB
or phone:
Scotland Tel (041) 357 1774
Northern Ireland Tel (0232) 244274

Support Groups

British Association for Early Childhood Education (BAECE)
Studio 3:2
140 Tabernacle Street
London EC2A 4SD
Tel (071) 250 1768
Information and book on childcare

Barnardo's
244/246 Harolds Cross Road
Dublin 6
Tel (01) 977276/977313
Childcare; Disadvantaged children

City Child
1 Bridgewater Sq
Barbican
London EC2
Tel (071) 374 0939
Advice on new nursery buildings

Pre-school Playgroups Association (PPA) (UK)
National Centre
61-63 King's Cross Road
london WC1x
Tel (071) 833 0991

Irish Pre-school Playgroups Association (IPPA)
Top Floor
19 Wicklow Street
Dublin 2
Tel (01) 719245

Industrial Society: Pepperell Unit
Robert Hyde House
48 Bryanston Square
London WIH 7LH
Tel (071) 262 2401
Campaigns for greater equality of opportunity in employment. Works with organisations in private and public sectors, with individuals and people in education. Provides training for managers in organisations to enable them to diversify and make more effective use of their resources.

National Children's Nurseries Association (NCNA)
Carmichael House
4 North Brunswick Street
Dublin 7
Advises on setting up child-minding schemes. Can also provide parents with information on child-minding.

872053

National Child-minding Association
8 Masons Hill
Bromley
Kent BR2 9EY
Tel (01) ??(check prefix) 464 6164
Advises employers on setting up child-minding schemes. Can also provide parents with information on child-minding.

COW or GATE
freephone
1800 - 570 570
free parents guide.

National Advisory Centre on Careers for Women
Artillery House
Artillery Row
London SW1
Tel (071) 799 2129
Provides career advice, encourages employers to fully utilise women's skills and offers women training opportunities.

Working Mother's Association
77 Holloway Road
London N7 8JZ
Tel (071) 700 5771
Provides local support network for working parents and encourages all relevant agencies and employers to improve working conditions for working mothers.

Workplace Nurseries Ltd
London SE1
Tel (071) 582 7199
Consultancy service to both trade unions and employers.

Book / Publications Distributors

Montessori Today
The Montessori Today Publishing Company
PO Box 4RB
London W1A 4RB

Nursery World Magazine
The School House Workshop
51 Calthorpe Street
London WC1 X OHH

Simon & Schuster
66 Wood Lane End
Hemel Hempstead
Herts HP2 4RG
Educational / Childcare Books

National Children's Bureau
8 Wakley Street
Islington
London EC1V 7QE
Tel (01) 278 9441
Information centre; Book sales - child care and related topics

---

Suppliers

St Nicholas Montessori Apparatus
22-24 Princes Gate
London SW7 1PT
Tel (071) 225 1277

Humpty Dumpty Club
Odhams Leisure Direct Ltd
147 Lower Drumcondra Road
Dublin 9
Tel 376690

Nimble Fingers
Toys/Equipment
Dublin Road
Stillorgan
Tel (01) 880788/880382

Nienhuis Montessori Material
Kilgarron House
Enniskerry
Co Wicklow
Tel (01) 829526 (evenings)

Evans
Art and School Supplies
24 Mary's Abbey
Dublin 7
Tel (01) 747511

Early Learning Centre
3 Henry St
Dublin 1
Tel (01) 731945

Early Learning Centre
Head Office
Hawksworth
Swindon
Wiltshire SN2 1TT
Tel (0793) 610171

The Red House Book Club
Witney
Oxon OX8 6YQ
Tel (0993) 71144/74171

Book Club of Ireland
Freepost
PO Box 1155
Crumlin
Dublin 12

Other Useful Addresses

Childcare Associates
Clifton House
54 Merrion Sq
Tel (01) 613788/615822
Fax 615200
*Childcare Consultants
Specialising in workplace
nurseries.*

Alan B Kidd & Co Ltd
Insurance Brokers
7 Palmerston Villas
Rathmines
Dublin 6
Phone 975465
*Specialist in day nursery
insurance.*

FAS Foras Aiseanna Saothair
D'Olier House
D'Olier Street
Dublin 2
Tel (01) 711544

Fire Prevention Council
32 Nassau Street
Dublin 2
Tel (01) 714070

Irish Red Cross Society
16 Merrion Square
Dublin 2
Tel (01) 765135

Revenue Commissioners
Castle House
South Great George's St
Dublin 2
Tel (01) 792777

National Safety Council
4 Northbrook Road
Ranelagh
Dublin 6
Tel (01) 963422

Recommended Reading

Some of these books may be expensive but a 'Nursery' copy would be of great benefit to staff.

General Childcare

Bowlby, John *Childcare and the Growth of Love* Pelican, London, 1953

Clarke-Stewart, Alison *Day Care: The Developing Child* Fontana, London, 1982

Leach, Penelope *Who Cares?* Penguin, London, 1979

Lentin, Ronit and Niland, Geraldine *Who's Minding the Children?* Arlen House, Dublin, 1980

Working Parents

Finch, Sue and Craigie, Penny *Practical Guide to Workplace Nurseries* Workplace Nurseries Ltd, London, 1990

Gieve, Katherine *Balancing Act: On Being a Working Mother* Virago, London, 1989

McKenna, Anne *Childcare and Equal Opportunities: Policies and Services for Childcare in Ireland* Employment Equality Agency, Dublin, 1988

Minimum Legal Requirements and Standards for Daycare Services for Children: Report of a Committe Appointed by the Minister for Health Stationery Office, Dublin, 1985

Velmans, Marianne and Litvinoff, Sarah *Working Mother: A Practical Handbook* Corgi, London, 1988

Waring, Marilyn *If Women Counted* MacMillan, London, 1989

Children Learning and Playing

Crowe, Brenda *Play is a Feeling* Unwin, London, 1984

Hendrick, Joanne *Total Learning: Curriculum for the Young Child* Merrill Publishing, USA, 1986

Holman and Bannett *Young Children in Action* High Scope, USA, 1979 (available from the National Children's Bureau)

Holt, John *How Children Fail* Pelican, London, 1969

Holt, John *How Children Learn* Pelican, London, 1984

Kellmer Pringle, Mia *The Needs of Children* Hutchinson, London, 1975

McLaughlin, B *Help Your Child Through Primary School* Mentor Publications, Ireland, 1986

Montessori, Maria *The Discovery of the Child* Clio Press, London, 1988

Thompson, Brenda *The Preschool Book* Unwin, London, 1980

Play Ideas

O'Donoghue, Miriam *Craft Book Series:*
Fun Crafts
Animal Crafts
Christmas Crafts
Mother's Day and Valentine's Day Crafts
Irish Crafts
Spring and Easter Crafts
Unique Publications, Dublin, 1989

Vogel, A *The Big Book for Growing Gardeners* Macmillan, London, 1982

Running Your Own Business

Attfield, Janet *The Business Side of Playgroups* PPA, England, 1980
(available from the Preschool Playgroups Associations of Ireland and of Britain)

Cashman, Aileen *Money Matters for Women* Attic Press, Dublin, 1989

Fleetwood, David and Pale, Alastair *Records and Book-Keeping in the Small Business* Irish Banks Standing Committee, Dublin, 1984
(available in banks in Ireland)

O'Connor, Joyce and Ruddle, Helen *Business Matters for Women* Attic Press, Dublin, 1990

Health and Nutrition

Duff, Gail *Healthy Food for Healthy Children* Conran Octopus, London, 1988

Food and Drink for the Under-Fives: Guidelines for officers-in-charge of under-fives facilities, catering staff and others involved in the day care of young children in Greater London The London Food Commission, London

Hanssen, Maurice *E for Additives* Thorsons, London, 1989

Stanway, Dr P *The Mothercare Guide to Child Health* Conran Octopus, London, 1988

Stoppard, Dr Miriam *The New Babycare and Child Medical Handbook* Dorling Kindersley, London, 1990

Stoppard, Dr Miriam *My first Food Book* Dorling Kindersley, London, 1987

Wilkes, Angela and Cartwright, Stephen *The Usborne First Cookbook* Usborne, London, 1984

Index